A Biographical Dictionary of the Twentieth-Century Royal Navy

A Biographical Dictionary
of the Twentieth-Century
Royal Navy

Volume 1 Admirals of the Fleet and Admirals

Alastair Wilson RN

Seaforth
PUBLISHING

Alastair Wilson © 2013

First published in Great Britain in 2013 by
Seaforth Publishing
An imprint of Pen & Sword Books Ltd
47 Church Street, Barnsley
S Yorkshire S70 2AS

www.seaforthpublishing.com
Email info@seaforthpublishing.com

British Library Cataloguing in Publication Data
A CIP data record for this book is available
from the British Library

ISBN 978-1-84832-088-8

Typeset and designed by M.A.T.S, Leigh-on-Sea, Essex
Printed in China through Printworks Int. Ltd.

Contents

A Note on the CD

The compact disk that accompanies this book is in pdf format so is designed to run best on Adobe® Acrobat®, whose Reader is widely installed on recent computers. For anyone without this software, it is available as a free download from the Adobe website. For UK-based readers this is

http://get.adobe.com/uk/reader/

With the CD in the drive, clicking on the pdf icon opens the file (it may be necessary to click on the CD icon first to reveal the pdf). It contains the records of 355 individuals in alphabetical order, and it is possible to scroll through the 1479 pages like a conventional book using the Adobe Reader's Forward and Back buttons. However, the contents list on pages 3-8 contains live links, so that clicking on a name opens the record for that individual; clicking on the surname at the head of the record returns the reader to the contents list.

The records are also fully searchable using Abobe Reader's Find command, so it is possible, for example, to look for ship names, people or even dates within the records. As it is a very large document, this may seem relatively slow, but it is probably faster than using a conventional book index.

While it is possible – and permissible – to print off individual records for convenience, the publishers would stress that the copying of the CD itself or the transmission of its contents is a breach of copyright.

Acknowledgements

IN compiling this record, I owe a very great deal to a number of people, who started off by being contacts, but have become friends. In something like chronological order of help received, they are: Brian Cuthbert of PC Computers, who provided the hardware, and kept it running; Roger Stratford of Rainshine, who produced the very special database program, which has required virtually no tweaking in about ten years; Peter Hore, who put me in touch with Seaforth; Allison, Heather and Margaret, the librarians at the National Museum of the Royal Navy; the library staff of Bognor Regis Public Library; the individual officers (one or two of whom have sadly now crossed the bar) who responded so promptly to my request that they check the entries I had compiled from the *Navy List* (and which showed that the *Navy List* is not always to be believed); and Andy Godfrey, of the RN Disclosure Cell, at Whale Island: without his help, these records would be a great deal less authoritative than I hope they are. Three other individuals are John Beattie (author of *Churchill's Scheme*), Jock Gardner (of the Naval Historical Branch), and Basil Watson (biographer of Admiral of the Fleet Lord Fieldhouse). And there are a number of any mouse ('in' naval joke) contributors to the Wardroom Bar online chatroom of the *Naval Review* who have come up with the missing piece of information I couldn't find anywhere else. E & OE, to whom I apologise.

Lastly, I owe more than I can say to my wife, Jill. I doubt very much that a husband closeted with a computer featured in her vision of the future when she said, 'I do,' over fifty-five years ago.

Introduction

IN the nineteenth century, there were two *Dictionaries of Naval Biography*, Marshall's (published 1823) and O'Byrne's (published 1849), in which latter this compiler's great-great-grandfather featured in a minor way. For naval historians of the twentieth century, there is no such equivalent, and it is hoped that this work will fill a need. Also it seems certain that the twentieth century will be the last one in which the Royal Navy played a major part in world history throughout the century, and it is suggested that a record of the careers of the men who made it what it was is worth having.

This compendium is intended for the amateur genealogist as much as for the amateur naval historian (and it is to be hoped that the professional will also find it useful). Therefore, the notes on the records are fairly extensive, with the aim of explaining such things as 'half pay', and commenting on the various sources from which this has been compiled.

For ease of handling the mass of data, it has been decided to divide it into several parts, based on the final rank achieved:

Volume 1   Admirals of the Fleet and Admirals
Volume 2   Vice-Admirals (in course of preparation)
Volume 3   Rear-Admirals (in outline at present)
Volume 4   Captains, Royal Navy
Volume 5   Commanders, Royal Navy
Volume 6   Lieutenant-Commanders, Royal Navy and below
                   (selected).

Volume 1 of the records is to be found on the CD inside the back cover.

In these biographical summaries, the criterion for the final rank classification has been that the officer concerned was on the Active List of the Royal Navy in that rank. It may have been for no more than a day, but if so, that counts. On the other hand, officers who were later promoted on the Retired List will appear in the list appropriate to the rank they held on retirement. A more detailed comment appears in the discussion of History and Context below.

The apparent lack of regard for the more junior officers is not intended as a slight, but is merely a recognition of the fact that their total numbers would produce a database of something like a quarter of a million names, and it is a fact that their influence has been in actions, rather than in higher management (because that is what junior-ranking officers do), and that, in consequence, their outstanding services have usually been in time of war, which occupies a comparatively small part of the century. Nor have officers of the Reserves been included, although many made significant contributions to British naval history in this century: again, it is a matter of time and space.

History and Context

ARGUABLY, the Royal Navy started the twentieth century at the zenith of its power, having reached that zenith eighty-five years earlier, at the end of the Great War against revolutionary and imperial France. During those eighty-five years navies had changed out of all recognition in materiel, and overall the Royal Navy had led the way in new developments. It had not always been the first to introduce some new equipment or material, but once having decided that something new was worth pursuing, the Royal Navy usually could out-build or out-develop all other nations. It had done so in 1859–61 with the introduction of the iron-hulled, iron-armoured battleship. It did so again in 1906 when the *Dreadnought* appeared.

Throughout the nineteenth century, a strong navy was seen as an indispensable arm of British foreign policy, and although there were moments in the 1880s under Gladstone's administrations when the political will to provide such a force might have seemed lacking, by and large government resources were made available to provide a navy adequate for the circumstances of the time.

The twentieth century opened with the naval arms race with Germany, which produced the two fleets that opposed each other in the North Sea in 1914–18. But at the same time, the USA quietly started to build a modern fleet, as did Japan, and until 1950 these four navies and the French were the fleets which mattered in world politics.

The year 1918 saw Britain exhausted, politically, socially and economically, and this was reflected in the 1922 Washington Treaty under which the USA was 'allowed' parity with the British fleet, with Japan close behind.

The two-power standard of the late-Victorian period (the ability to match, in naval terms, the two next largest naval powers put together) had given way to a one-power standard prior to the First World War, and now to no more than parity. Eighteen years later, the Second World War, in naval terms, was less about command of the oceans than it was about logistics (to use a later word). Germany was never going to be defeated by a purely maritime policy, but the supply of food, men and materials across the Atlantic bridge was the crucial battle which had to be won if the Allies were to defeat Nazi Germany in the land battle. In the Pacific, imperial Japan was defeated by logistics, supplying men and equipment to push the empire inwards, and denying that empire the sinews of war for itself.

If 1918 was a year of exhaustion for Britain, 1945 was more so. The changes started during the First World War continued during the Second, and at the end of the first half of the century, the Royal Navy was unquestionably smaller in size than the US Navy. Thereafter, the decline continued, with the Soviet Union building a formidable navy (which was never put to the test before it was broken and neglected with the downfall of the USSR at the end of the century). As radio and the conquest of the air effectively shrank the world in size, and as the nations of the British Empire became independent, the need for an all-powerful navy lessened. Under the perceived threat of Soviet Russia, the Royal Navy concentrated on the North Atlantic, although, possibly more by good luck than good judgement, it retained sufficient worldwide capacity to fight the Falklands campaign of 1982.

At the end of the twentieth century, the United States' navy has become the sole arbiter of world sea-power. The only other navies capable of serious worldwide operations in virtually all fields of naval warfare are the British and French navies, though forward-looking strategists are watching China and India with interest.

In Britain, since the Glorious Revolution of 1688, the armed forces have always submitted to political control, and in the twentieth century there were few naval officers who took any serious part in politics while they were still in a position to influence naval events. (Sir John Fisher, although never a Member of Parliament, was one such. So too was Lord Charles Beresford, who was an MP – he was the younger son of a peer, and so could be an MP – but his contribution was more nuisance value than positive.) So the decline of Britain's naval power has not been due to any shortcomings of the naval direction, but has been in response to political decisions, which largely followed economic realities.

Nonetheless, Britain remains one of the world's largest economies (to quote a ranking is pointless, since they change all the time), with world-wide trading links. And over 90 per cent of that trade comes and goes by sea. Seaborne trade is vulnerable to all sorts of dangers: it is said that there are no more than seven 'choke points' (e.g. the straits of Gibraltar, the Malacca straits, etc) through which 90 per cent of world trade passes. So Britain's national well-being still relies on the sea and trade – a fact of which most British politicians and much of the British public seem blithely unaware – and a strong navy, firmly handled, is still an essential, if largely unseen, tool of government.

The senior naval officers whose biographical summaries appear here were, or are, the products of a period stretching back to the 1850s (for the Admirals at the start of the century) up to the 1970s (for the Commanders and Captains at the end of the century). Their actions reflect the developments of that period. Their successors will build on the actions of their twentieth-century mentors.

Coverage of the Entries

The prime aim of these biographical notes is to provide skeleton details of each subject's career in the Royal Navy: his seniority in the ranks he held; a list of ships and establishments he served in and the date on which he was appointed; and what those ships were and where they served. The amount of detail varies slightly, because the different sources consulted have themselves varied during the century – see note 11, Sources.

Entry

Commissioned officers of the Royal Navy are, and nearly always have been, drawn from the middle class of British society. There have been younger sons of the lesser nobility and of the landed gentry, and at the opposite end of the social scale there have been many self-educated men who have made their way to the top. But, by and large, career naval officers throughout the twentieth century have been drawn from the professional classes. (There are, of course, many exceptions to prove the rule – a notable one being Admiral of the Fleet Sir Caspar John, First Sea Lord in the 1960s, who was the son of the very bohemian painter Augustus John – though the latter was himself the son of a solicitor).

At the start of the twentieth century, there was virtually no opportunity for a man from the lower deck to join the ranks of commissioned officers. The first such organized scheme was introduced by Winston Churchill when he was First Lord (the political head of the Navy) in 1912. In 1900 all officers joined at the age of 12–14 via the training ship HMS *Britannia*, shortly to be moved ashore. In fact, at the outset of the century virtually all officers but the most senior had been through the *Britannia* mill. Prior to that, a young man obtained a nomination from a Flag Officer, passed a rudimentary exam in the three Rs, and then joined a ship for some six years of extremely practical training. The process of nomination meant that it was largely a matter of knowing the right people that produced a scarcely-changing breed of naval officer.

The *Britannia*, and the College which succeeded the ship, both educated and trained the young men, and so it remained until 1955. Thereafter, officers joined the Navy when they had completed their academic education, and increasingly this meant having achieved an academic degree, so that at the end of the century, taking a page from the *Navy List 2000* at random, 36 out of the 63 names on the page, from Rear-Admiral to Sub-Lieutenant, had a degree; while out of the 36 officers on the active Flag List, 12 had degrees.

Entry to the *Britannia* was by competitive exam and interview, so nepotism was less effective – though it could help you to achieve promotion once in the Navy. In 1913 the Navy instituted a scheme of entry for boys who had completed their education at public or grammar schools (the 'Special Entry') which ran in parallel with the Dartmouth entry until 1955. These forms of entry were supplemented in times of crisis by recruiting from the Royal Naval Reserve – particularly at the end of the nineteenth century when the original 'hungry hundred' were recruited, and again in 1938 with the expansion for the soon-to-come World War bringing the need for many more officers. From 1912 onwards young ratings of promise from the lower deck could become 'Upper Yardmen', and in due course sub-lieutenants with unlimited career opportunities: many have achieved Flag rank. And in the aftermath of the Second World War, many officers who had gained temporary commissions in the Royal Naval Volunteer Reserve transferred to regular commissions in the Royal Navy: some of them, too, went to the very top, with more than one reaching the rank of Admiral.

Prior to 1955 the average age at which a young officer entered the fleet, having completed his education and basic training, was 20–21. Thereafter the age has risen steadily, until by 2000 the average age was about 24 – reflecting the time at university, and also the larger number of officers who joined the unified list of officers from the lower deck.

Rank structure

The Royal Navy has a hierarchical structure, from the youngest Boy Seaman up to Admiral of the Fleet. In theory, an individual could rise from the former to the latter, and although none did so, some went from Ordinary Seaman (one step above a Boy) to Admiral (one below Admiral of the Fleet). The largest part of the Navy's officer corps has entered the service halfway up the ladder, at the bottom of the commissioned officers' hierarchy. In the twentieth century this has been achieved by selection based on a combination of educational achievements and interview, the techniques and details of which have varied over the years, depending on the fashionable ideas prevailing.

There has been no real change in the hierarchical structure in the twentieth century, and it is as follows.

Rank	Approximate Age	How achieved
(Naval) Cadet	13–17	Competitive examination & interview. Until the introduction of the Special Entry in 1913, all Cadets, whether in the old *Britannia* or the College(s) or at sea in the fleet, were referred to as 'Naval Cadets'. Thenceforward, they remained Naval Cadets while training ashore, but Cadet, Cadet (E) or Cadet (S) when once they went to sea, either in one of the various training ships or in the fleet
Midshipman	16–19	Automatically on successful completion of Cadet's training.
Sub-Lieutenant	19–23	On completion of minimum time as a Midshipman, and passing certain examinations. This was also the rank at which a man promoted from the lower deck entered the officer hierarchy.
Lieutenant	22–45 (before 1914)	Promotion to Lieutenant's rank was dependent on successful completion of Lieutenant's courses, taken at the specialist schools in Portsmouth while an Acting Sub-Lieutenant. At the start of the century, they were Gunnery, Torpedo and Navigation (and, of course, Seamanship, the examination for which was taken at the end of one's time as a Midshipman). Depending on the classes of pass one obtained in the examinations, one could obtain additional seniority in the rank of Lieutenant. On completion of courses one went to sea as a confirmed Sub-Lieutenant to gain a Bridge Watchkeeping Certificate (BWK). (At the

beginning of the century this was known as a Certificate of Competency.) It was generally held that this could not be gained in less than six months' sea-time, but there was a degree of flexibility, which depended on one's Captain.

Lieutenant	22–32 (after 1914)	Before 1914, the rank of Lieutenant-Commander did not exist. Promotion to Commander was by selection at an average age of 37. From 1914 onwards, Lieutenants were promoted automatically to the rank of Lieutenant-Commander on attaining eight years' seniority as a Lieutenant.
Lieutenant-Commander	30–45	This was the highest rank which could be reached without undergoing a further selection process. An officer 'passed over' for promotion could (and for the first three-quarters of the century usually did) remain in the Service until he reached the compulsory retiring age (45 until 1956, 50 thereafter). The retirement age varied with rank.
Commander	33–53	Promotion from Lieutenant-Commander to Commander, and from Commander to Captain was by a further selection process, after some four years in the rank. If not promoted, then the compulsory retiring age for Commanders was 50 until 1956, thereafter 53.
Captain	37–55	For Captains, the next step was to Rear-Admiral. Failure to be selected for Flag rank resulted in compulsory retirement after nine years' service, or at age 55, whichever came earlier.
[Commodore]		Throughout the century, until 1999, Commodore was NOT a *rank* in the Royal Navy (although a BBC 'Mastermind' question in the 1980s, 'What, in the Royal Navy, is the next rank above Captain?' incorrectly gave 'Commodore' as the answer). A Commodore was an *appointment*, where a senior Captain was given a temporary authority to exercise command over a group of ships. On completion of that appointment, he reverted to his previous rank of Captain. There were originally a Commodore 1st Class, and a Commodore 2nd Class. The distinction was abolished in 1956. (In 1999, Commodore became a rank, to equate with a Brigadier or Air Commodore.)
Rear-Admiral	48–60	Rear-Admirals rarely flew their flag for more than two appointments in the rank. It was a case of 'up or out'.
Vice-Admiral	50–65	The same applied to Vice-Admirals.
Admiral	52–65	And for Admirals.

Admiral of the Fleet	65–70	It was rare for an Admiral of the Fleet to be employed on the Active List, though it was more common in the first half of the century. Until 1940, Admirals of the Fleet were placed on the Retired List at the age of 70 (though there were exceptions – Sir Henry Keppel, at the start of the century, remained on the Active List until his death at the age of 95). After February 1940, they remained nominally on the Active List until their death. This resulted in a higher number of Admirals of the Fleet on the Active List than there had been in the earlier part of the century.

The average ages and comments above should not be considered as inviolable: the rules and ages altered slightly in the course of the century. In wartime especially, officers were sometimes promoted early as a reward for meritorious conduct (Admiral of the Fleet Earl Beatty received his promotion to Commander at the age of only 28). And officers of Flag rank were retained for longer than would have been the case in peacetime.

Also, officers nominally on the Retired List were brought back for active service, but remained on the Retired List (and thus were not eligible for promotion to the substantive higher rank). Vice-Admiral Sir James Somerville had been placed on the Retired List for medical reasons just before the outbreak of war in 1939, but spent a most strenuous war at sea, with two major sea commands (Force 'H' and the Eastern Fleet), before his services were recognized by his restoration to the Active List (and promotion to Admiral of the Fleet).

Nor was it unknown for officers to be promoted more than one rank at a time, though this was infrequent. Two examples were: Lord Louis Mountbatten (as he then was) who went straight from Captain to Acting Vice-Admiral in 1942, and Admiral Sir Nigel Essenhigh who jumped from Rear-Admiral to Admiral in 1998.

Promotion up to Captain's rank

Until the very end of the twentieth century, however you entered the ranks of commissioned officers in the Navy, your promotion to Lieutenant (later Lieutenant-Commander) was automatic and assured. Without further promotion, one might have a satisfying career to the age of 45 (50 from

1956), having had command of a small ship, or ships, or a responsible training appointment, or on an operational staff. Selection for those plum jobs depended on your ability, but their satisfactory performance was no guarantee that you would be promoted further.

Promotion to Commander was the step that counted, and was entirely by selection, based on reports written by your captain. The exact method by which selections were made developed throughout the century, but by and large the system was seen as being fair, and while it sometimes passed over good men, it very rarely allowed men of lesser calibre to be promoted – there were too many checks and balances. Seniority in the lower rank was a minor factor, but it counted insofar as an officer was competing for promotion with his contemporaries and near-contemporaries.

The same system applied in selection for promotion to Captain. This was the senior rank in which one might have direct, personal, and everyday contact with the lower deck. These were the men who 'set the tone' of the Navy. To command one of HM's ships called for substantial leadership qualities and a total knowledge of one's profession.

Promotion to Flag rank

In Nelson's navy, once you were 'made post', that is, had reached the rank of Captain, you were assured of ultimately becoming an Admiral, so long as you survived. Promotion to the Flag List (the list of officers entitled to fly an Admiral's flag, whether Rear-, Vice-, or full Admiral) was solely dependent on seniority, as was your progression up the list.

At the start of the twentieth century, matters had changed slightly. To achieve Flag rank you had to have reached the top of the Captains' List (pure seniority), but you also had to have served a specified length of time in command at sea as a Captain. If you met those criteria, then when your turn came, you were promoted to Rear-Admiral. If not, you were placed on the Retired List. Once on the Flag List, you might not be employed, but you remained on the Active List, theoretically likely to fly your flag. If you were not chosen, then you were retired after about seven years. Much the same rules applied for promotion to Vice-Admiral and Admiral.

At the end of the First World War, the system was further refined: on reaching the top of the Captains' List, with sufficient sea-time, you were automatically promoted to Rear-Admiral, but, unless you were going to be given an appointment more or less immediately, you were placed on the Retired List one day later, but you could say that you were a Rear-Admiral (and indeed, you could advance up the rank structure, becoming Vice-Admiral and Admiral on the Retired List).

This more or less automatic promotion, followed by retirement, was halted during the Second World War, when Admiral Pound, the then First Sea Lord, wished to promote younger men to the Flag List. So, at the same time as promotions to Rear-Admiral started to be taken from those who had not yet reached the top of the Captain's List, automatic promotion to Rear-Admiral on the Active List ceased. However, Captains who reached the top of their list without being promoted could still be promoted to Retired Rear-Admiral, etc.

Similar conditions prevailed in the Engineering and Accountant (Paymaster) branches in the same period, although the incidence of one-day promotions to the Flag List was smaller; substantial numbers of Engineer and Paymaster Captains were 'placed on the Retired List and promoted Engineer (Paymaster) Rear-Admiral'.

Throughout this period, the number of Flag Officers at any one time was limited by the total establishment agreed with the Treasury, and varied from time to time as the size of the fleet varied.

Half pay

The rationale for half pay is well explained in *The Navy of Britain*.[1] It was introduced by Charles II as a means of retaining the services of a corps of professional sea-officers. While the State recognized that there would be times when it would have no immediate use for its sea-officers (and it certainly wasn't going to pay them the full rate for doing nothing), it also realized that if it didn't pay them a retaining fee, then when the time came that their services were required they might not be available. Charles II's measures were very limited in their application, applying only to certain captains, and for a limited period; but the principle was established, and by 1693, half pay applied to virtually all the commissioned officer corps.

There were minor alterations made during the eighteenth century (few, if any, erring on the generous side to the recipients), but throughout the eighteenth and nineteenth centuries, members of the officer corps of the Royal Navy were paid full pay when they were employed in one of HM Ships, and half pay when they weren't. Since there was no Manpower Planning in those days, there were usually many more officers at all levels than there were seagoing appointments (except, of course, in time of war). Thus, if one wanted to make one's way in the Royal Navy in peacetime, it helped greatly to have 'interest' (a friend, or network of friends and relations, who could drop a word in the appropriate ear) to enable one to receive an appointment. Financially, this might have double advantages; first, one received full pay, and in wartime one might receive prize money.

1 *The Navy of Britain*, Professor Michael Lewis (George Allen & Unwin, London, 1948), p.258ff.

In peacetime, though, opportunities for employment were few and far between, and in the nineteenth century very many naval officers spent more time on half pay than they did on full pay. (A glance at O'Byrne's *Dictionary of Naval Biography*[2] will reveal this – O'Byrne opens each entry with 'F-P *x* years: H-P *y* years'.) And these entries will show that the 1860s in particular were a lean period – many of the officers listed here, who may be said to be the cream since they went on to achieve post and then Flag rank, spent up to four years at a stretch without an appointment. This meant that on the Flag List there was a fair amount of 'Buggins' turn', and inexperienced officers received appointments for which they were scarcely suited, while more competent officers kicked their heels in idleness. Nonetheless, the right men usually managed to turn up in the right job at the right time.

Financially, the system meant that most naval officers had to possess some private means of their own – otherwise they could barely have supported their families while on half pay, but two instances may be quoted of the effects that came from it. In 1879–81, a 'Flying Squadron' was sent on a round-the-world trip (among the young officers were Prince Albert Victor and Prince George, later HM King George V). In the event, having sailed east-about and reached Japan, they turned round and returned the way they came. Admiral George Ballard, then a Midshipman, wrote later:[3]

> ... the stage in our long cruise was reached at which the three vessels forming the remnant of the last of the Flying Squadrons were on the point of departure from Singapore round the Cape of Good Hope to Europe, which all hands were hoping would prove for home. ... till our arrival off Anjer Head in the morning, on the east side of the Straits of Sunda, where we anchored for a few hours preparatory to being out of sight of any land whatever for at least a month or more to come. ... we only did anchor because on departing from Singapore the Admiral had been told to enquire for possible telegraphic orders ... it was even rumoured in the squadron that the Admiral now received the option of returning by the Suez route [which would have been substantially shorter and quicker] though that may have been wishful thinking. But something of a nature never divulged was almost certainly discussed on board the flagship, for the captains of the other vessels were signalled for and remained a long time. If it really was the case that they had a choice of route under consideration their preference for the longer one was almost a foregone conclusion. All three captains happened to be

2 *Dictionary of Naval Biography*, W.R. O'Byrne, London, 1849 (there is a modern reprint, Savannah Publications, 1990).

3 The *Naval Review*, November 1941, p.616.

bachelors with no strong domestic ties; and in these days when half pay was the curse of the upper ranks of the Service, no captain looked forward to paying off unless for some special reason. The inducement for the Admiral to prefer the Cape route was stronger still, as he had hoisted his flag for the first time only two months before, after a long wait on a rear-admiral's half pay of only £450 a year. …

The second instance concerns the author's own family: his great-great-great grandfather, the latter's son, and his son in turn, were not particularly distinguished middle-ranking officers in the Victorian Navy. The first two were Executive Officers, one a retired Commander, the other a Captain, but the last became an officer of the Navigating Branch, which barred him from ever commanding one of HM's warships, but did promise more or less continuous employment on full pay as a hydrographic surveyor, as indeed proved to be the case, and he rose to be a Staff-Captain without ever being on half pay, which would not have happened had he been an executive officer.

For most of the eighteenth and nineteenth centuries there was no formalized system of retirement: when once an officer had received his commission, he remained a sea-officer liable (in theory, anyway) to be recalled for service until the day he died. Thus Admirals were appointed when aged into their seventies and even eighties. And since promotion to Captain ensured that, provided one lived long enough, promotion through the Flag List by seniority was inevitable, there was substantial over-crowding in the upper echelons of the *Navy List*. A few half-hearted efforts were made to make officers retire, and so free up the list for younger men to be promoted, and retired pay was introduced which was similar in amount to half pay, but not so attractive if one nursed any hopes of further employment and promotion.

However, by 1900 the rules were fairly well established, with officers receiving full pay while in employment and half pay when not, and fixed ages for retirement, depending on rank. One consequence of the whole concept of half pay, descending from the very earliest days, was that an officer could decide not to take up an appointment, and remain on half pay if he so wished. In the days when paid holidays for everyone, as part of one's contract of employment, were unheard of, leave for officers was entirely at the whim of one's Commanding Officer: there was no allowance of annual leave in the *Navy List* or Queen's Regulations and Admiralty Instructions. The only leave allowance was for those returning from foreign service.

The half-pay regulations in 1900 stated, inter alia:

that officers would be placed on the half-pay list 'as soon as his Full-pay ceases and his accounts are clear';

that officers returning from foreign service were 'entitled to leave of absence on Full-pay';

that 'An officer taking passage out in a Mail Packet or Private Ship will reckon Foreign Service from date of embarcation for passage out' [which is why, in the records, particularly in the years up to 1914, Flag Officers taking up an appointment will be found sometimes to have two dates – the date of their appointment, when they took passage, and went on to full pay, and the one given when, after arrival on the foreign station, they hoisted their flag; officers at home started their full pay on the day they hoisted their flag];

that 'An officer returning to England, if entitled to Full-pay leave after arrival is to be borne on the book [*sic*] of the Flag-ship at whichever port is most convenient to him.'

Foreign Service Leave was granted on the following scale: for every complete six months, one week, and one additional day for each complete month of a period less than six months; thus, if one was away from home for three years, ten months and two days, one's leave entitlement on full pay would be seven weeks and four days; thereafter one went on half pay until reappointed. One exception was that if an officer had an official residence allocated to him (e.g. Admiral Superintendent of Malta Dockyard), then there was no entitlement to full pay leave.

In the 1920s, there was a differentiation between half pay and 'unemployed pay'. The regulations for half pay in 1930 stated, inter alia: 'Midshipmen, Mates and Sub-Lieutenants of all Branches not to be discharged to Half-Pay except for misconduct or at own request ...'

Under the heading 'Unemployed Pay', the regulations stated: 'In the case of Lieutenants, Lieutenant-Commanders and Commanders of all Branches, a distinction is drawn between Officers waiting employment and holding themselves at the disposal of the Admiralty, and those who are unemployed at their own request or in consequence of misconduct.'

The following table shows the different rates of pay (daily rates):

Rank	Full Pay	Unemployed Pay*	Half Pay
Lieutenant			
On promotion	17s 0d	17s 0d	8s 0d
After 4 years	£1 0s 0d	17s 0d	10s 0d
After 6 years	£1 4s 0d	17s 0d	12s 0d
Lieut.-Commander			
On promotion	£1 10s 0d	£1 2s 6d	15s 0d
After 3 years	£1 12s 0d	£1 2s 6d	16s 0d
After 6 years	£1 14s 0d	£1 2s 6d	17s 0d
Commander			
On promotion	£2 0s 0d	£1 7s 6d	£1 0s 0d

*Full rate paid for six months: then next six months as below – after total of one year – half-pay.

From which it will be seen that half pay was exactly what it said. And a newly promoted Commander, who wasn't immediately employed in his new rank, was paid full rate as a Commander from the first day of his promotion.

Captains were treated slightly differently, and less advantageously. If they left one appointment without another to go to immediately, they were not kept on full pay for the first six months, but went immediately on to unemployed pay. If they were newly promoted, this effectively meant that their pay stood still, at the same rate as they had been paid as a Commander. If they had been employed in the rank of Captain, then they received an immediate drop in pay.

Half pay finally disappeared, to all intents and purposes, in 1938. There was a substantial improvement in officers' pay and conditions with the introduction of Marriage Allowance and the abolition of half pay. Thereafter, from the day you entered Dartmouth until the day you retired, you were paid the rate for your rank. However, half pay was retained, and remained at the end of the twentieth century, for Admirals of the Fleet and for officers who had been disciplined by being Dismissed their Ship, until they were reappointed.

One result of this system (if it can be so described) is that at the start of the century, there were 74 Flag Officers on the Active List (5 Admirals of the Fleet, 9 Admirals, 22 Vice-Admirals and 38 Rear-Admirals). Of these, 29 were in full-pay appointments, while the remainder, 45, or 60 per cent, were on half pay.

In 1938, the last year in which half pay was paid, the figures were: total Flag Officers, 66 (3 Admirals of the Fleet, 10 Admirals, 20 Vice-Admirals and 33 Rear-Admirals). Of these, 42 were in full-pay appointments, while the remainder, 24, or 36 per cent, were on half pay.

At the end of 2000, there were 44 Flag Officers on the Active List: 7 Admirals of the Fleet (plus one 'former First Sea Lord'); 4 Admirals, 7 Vice-Admirals and 25 Rear-Admirals. Of these, *all* Admirals and below were in current appointments – though it has to be said that some of their titles would have raised eyebrows among the sea-officers of a century earlier: 'Capability Manager (Strategic Deployment)' and 'Team Leader Defence Training Review'. None of the Admirals of the Fleet were in (naval) employment.

It had become the custom for successive First Sea Lords to be promoted to Admiral of the Fleet on their last day in office. One or two (e.g. Fieldhouse) went on to be Chief of the Defence Staff as Admiral of the Fleet, but the remainder, effectively, then 'retired'. In 1997 the government decreed that the rank of Admiral of the Fleet (and its Army and RAF equivalents) should be 'put into abeyance'. But the Admiralty Board decided that ex-First Sea Lords, even if nominally only Admirals, should continue to enjoy the privileges they would have had, were it not for those killjoy politicians! Later still, former Chiefs and Vice-Chiefs of the Defence Staff were added. So the category 'ex-Chiefs of Defence Staff, First Sea Lord and Vice-Chief of Defence Staff who Remain on the Active List' now appears in the *Navy List*, on the Active List, between Admirals of the Fleet, and Admirals.

Retirement

Throughout the century, officers of all ranks were placed on the Retired List on reaching a certain age, which varied with the rank they held – some examples have been cited above.

In 1901 there were many more officers on the (nominally) Active Flag List than there were appointments, and in between appointments a Flag Officer would be placed on half pay. It was almost universal for a newly-promoted Flag Officer to be placed on half pay until an appointment became vacant. The rationale was that one could only be on full pay if one was appointed to a ship in a complement billet. Once promoted, one could not fill the billet previously occupied in the lower rank (the Admiralty couldn't countenance having a Rear-Admiral doing a Captain's job at a Rear-Admiral's rate of pay), so one received one's step, but (more or less) immediately gave up the previous appointment and its emoluments, and went on half pay, until such time as merit, influence, or 'Buggins' turn' brought an appointment. (But see above – between the First and Second World Wars, there was 'Unemployed Pay' for Commanders and below, which lay somewhere between half and full pay.)

To qualify for promotion to the next rung of the ladder, one had to have had a specified period in a Captain's appointment (for promotion to Rear-Admiral) or to have had a Flag appointment (to move up to the next rank on the Admirals' lists), and to have become the senior officer in your rank. If, say, a Rear-Admiral had not hoisted his flag (through lack of opportunity or 'interest' in securing an appointment) when he reached the top of the Rear-Admiral's list and a vacancy for a Vice-Admiral occurred, he would be placed on the Retired List, even though he might still be under the nominal retiring age. Details of the promotion rules applicable in 1900 will be found below under note 2, Seniority on the Active List.

In these biographical summaries, the criterion for the final rank classification has been that the officer concerned was on the Active List of the Royal Navy in that rank. It may have been for no more than a day, but if so, that counts. In the years before the First World War, there were many officers who became an Admiral for less than a week. However, there were also some officers who were placed on the Retired List on the same day as they were promoted. They are counted as having been promoted on the Retired List, and so will appear as having their final rank as the lower one, though any subsequent promotion on the Retired List will be recorded in the appropriate note.

Up until 1956, having been retired, one could still advance up the (retired) Flag List. And so, an officer, who retired as a 'mere' Rear-Admiral, could be promoted to Vice-Admiral on the Retired List, and Admiral on the Retired List, and be entitled to be addressed as such, although he had never served in that rank on the Active List. During the two World Wars, a number of such officers volunteered to serve, and appeared in the Active List alphabetical section of the *Navy Lists* in their higher rank. In that section their rank was given as the higher rank they held on the Retired List, but in the column headed 'seniority' there was no date, merely the word '*Retd.*'. Nor did they appear in the seniority section of the Active List, because they were no longer eligible for further promotion on the Active List. Thus, although it might be argued that they have served on the Active List in their higher rank, they have *not* been classified as having so served, because they were not *in all respects* members of the Active List.

There were, though, a few officers who had been placed on the Retired List who were recalled to serve in the Second World War, and who were subsequently restored to the Active List – Admirals Somerville and Ramsay are two examples. They are treated as though their careers had ended after their restoration to the Active List.

Conclusion

In almost every aspect of the foregoing pages it will probably be possible
to find some exception – the administration of the Royal Navy can be
flexible when it wants to be.

Background to the Biographical Entries

ALL the entries for each officer are laid out in the same format. The headings of the format are all in black; the information is in blue. All the headings with information attached are underlined. If a heading is not underlined, it is not applicable, or the information is not available.

The Reference Number (Ref No) at the head of each entry relates to the computer database on which all the information is stored, and is of no direct relevance in using the CD-ROM. However, it does indicate the initial letter of the subject's surname, his final rank (01 – Admiral of the Fleet; 02 – Admiral; 03 – Vice-Admiral) and a sequential number for his seniority from the start of the century (e.g. Admiral Sir Peter Abbott is A-02-00272).

Text within quotation marks, unless otherwise identified, is taken from the subject's service record.

Place names are as they were at the time (e.g. Peking, Pekin, Ceylon, etc.).

Readers who are pedantically inclined may cavil at the (apparently) excessive use of Capitals – but the Navy (the Royal Navy, that is, as opposed to any old navy) always has been prodigal and not entirely logical in their use. And the Navy has always, for no obvious reason, named four ships *Curacoa* rather than the correct *Curaçao*. (The name occurs quite frequently, and no, the text is correct!)

The editor of this compendium started with the intention of not using abbreviations and initials, but soon found that doing so would increase the length substantially so, reluctantly, he has given up, but has provided what it is hoped is a comprehensive decode.

1 Form of Entry

Nomination

At the start of the twentieth century, most officers had entered as Cadets in the old *Britannia*, moored in the river at Dartmouth. There were still some (Admiral of the Fleet Lord Fisher was one), who had entered under the age-old scheme of getting a nomination from a Flag Officer. (There had been minor changes to the regulations regarding nominations, but in essence Nelson got his start at sea by this means.)

Britannia

From August 1857, a training ship (originally the *Illustrious*) was established at Portsmouth to provide the basic training for Naval Cadets, who had entered with the express purpose of becoming naval officers, in a career which could lead them to the highest ranks. At that time, although they did exist, the opportunities for promotion from the lower deck were probably lower than at any time before or since, and the chances of such an officer achieving the highest rank were infinitesimally small. *Illustrious* was replaced by *Britannia*, and in February 1862 her station was moved to Portland. In October 1863, she moved to Dartmouth, which thus became the 'cradle of Neptune' (to borrow the title of a book). Cadets entered at the age of approximately 12½ and spent two years in the ship, before joining the Fleet. This system lasted, with amendments, until the Fisher-Selborne reforms of 1903, which instituted a four-year course. Before this was initiated, the building of a new college ashore at Dartmouth had been started, to take the place of the old *Britannia* (to which the *Hindostan* had been added). Since this building was only designed to take two years' worth of cadets, additional accommodation had to be found, and this was provided in a purpose-built, but temporary, set of buildings in the grounds of the royal estate of Osborne, in the Isle of Wight.

Osborne

From late 1903, and for some eighteen years thereafter, Naval Cadets entered the Royal Navy at the age of 12½–13 via the college at Osborne, where they spent two years before moving on to the Royal Naval College at Dartmouth (RNC Dartmouth) to complete their four-year course.

Special Entry

In 1913, it was decided to supplement the cadets who were educated at Osborne and Dartmouth with a number of 'Special Entry' cadets, who joined the navy after completion of their education at the age of 17½. Initially, they were known to their contemporaries as 'Pubs' (for public school), but the expression did not last very long. They did a short course of a year of exclusively naval training, and then joined the fleet as Midshipmen at the same time as their contemporaries who had spent four years at Osborne and Dartmouth. A great deal of ink was wasted in arguing the merits of the two schemes, but they worked successfully together for over forty years, and there will not be found a preponderance of one entry over another in the higher ranks. There were various sub-sets of the Special Entries, such as Direct Entry from the Merchant Navy Colleges, Pangbourne, HMS *Worcester* and HMS *Conway* (whose students were officially Cadets in the Royal Naval Reserve).

RNC Dartmouth (13)

RNC Dartmouth was opened in 1905, taking over from the old *Britannia*. By 1920 additional accommodation had been built at Dartmouth, and it was possible to close Osborne, and cadets then went to Dartmouth at the age of 12½–13 for the full four-year course (actually, eleven terms for most of the period); from 1920 to 1948, naval cadets were either 'Darts' or 'Special Entries'. Included among the 'Darts' from 1939 onwards were cadets who had entered under the 'Alexander' scheme, which gave an opportunity to boys from grammar schools to become naval officers. Between the years 1942–46, the College was evacuated from Dartmouth (after a German air-raid); first, and very briefly, terms 1–7 went to Bristol, then all eleven terms were moved to the Duke of Westminster's estate at Eaton Hall, near Chester. The course of training remained the same, and those who were trained at Eaton Hall are not differentiated as to form of entry.

RNC Dartmouth (16)

The Attlee government (1945–51) wished to widen the social field from which naval cadets were drawn, and in 1948 the Admiralty introduced another entry at age 16, which was intended to make it easier for boys at secondary modern and grammar schools to become officers when they had finished the standard state education (school-leaving age being then 15). May 1948 saw the first of the 16-year-old entry go to Dartmouth, while the last 13-year-old entry joined in May 1949, passing out in April 1953. So for five years there were three types of officer entry running concurrently.

COST Scheme (Committee on Officers' Structure and Training)

In 1955, naval officers' training was given another thorough overhaul, and entry was concentrated at age 17½, when all, whether the product of state or private schools, would have completed their academic education, and could be trained for the Navy under a common scheme, lasting nearly four years, including time at sea in the fleet. This scheme in turn lasted a fairly short time, and in the 1960s schemes were instituted to take university graduates into the Royal Navy. (The scheme was sometimes known – though not officially – as 'Completely Outdated Scheme of Training': it was not well-regarded in the fleet, it being held that it produced young officers inadequately prepared for life as a Naval officer. Thus the scheme's life was short.)

Murray Scheme

In 1958, another committee under the chairmanship of Sir Keith Murray (later Lord Murray of Newhaven), then Chairman of the University Grants Committee, was set up to re-examine the question of officer entry, and the scheme which bears Murray's name started in September 1960. The same principle, that entrants would have completed their academic education, applied, but with the expansion of university education generally, and the Navy's perceived need for degree-trained officers, the scheme was adjusted over the years to include entrants who had a university place, and who wished to be able to take it up, and also entrants who had obtained their degree. The Murray Scheme lasted until the end of 1973, and was replaced by the Naval College Entry.

NCE

The Naval College Entry were 17½-year old cadets who, on the whole, were not academically inclined. Their training period was the shortest of all, but some could be, and were, selected to go to university after they had joined Dartmouth.

UCE

The University Cadet Entry consisted of graduates who had decided during, or after, their time at university, that they would join the Royal Navy. In broad terms, at the end of the twentieth century, this is the main form of entry for officers who are likely to achieve the highest rank.

DGE

The Direct Graduate Entry was introduced in 1972. Young men with suitable degrees who passed a selection board entered as Acting Sub-Lieutenants, and after a short time at Dartmouth went to sea as Acting Sub-Lieutenants. They took their Fleet Board at the end of eighteen months, and then did Sub-Lieutenants' courses to qualify them for the rank of Lieutenant. Their seniority as a Lieutenant could be backdated substantially, depending on the class of degree they obtained, and the marks they were awarded at their Fleet Board.

Ex-RNVR

During the Second World War the Royal Navy had a requirement for an enormous number of young men to become officers, but only for the duration of the war. All were entered as ordinary sailors, and after a short period at sea became officers, with temporary Royal Naval Volunteer Reserve commissions. At the end of the war a number were offered permanent commissions in the Royal Navy, and some went on to achieve very high rank. And in the immediate post-war period up until 1961, when universal national service was the rule, a number of young men were similarly commissioned into the RNVR, and were likewise offered permanent commissions.

Ex-RNR

Exactly the same applied to the RNR. Merchant service officers, holding commissions in the Royal Naval Reserve, were similarly offered commissions in the Royal Navy.

Lower deck

In 1912, when Winston Churchill was First Lord of the Admiralty, the 'Mate' scheme was introduced, to take promising ratings who had adequate educational attainments and give them a special course, and promote them to Sub-Lieutenant. The idea was to select them sufficiently young (under the age of 25 on being commissioned) so that they could compete on equal terms with the 'Darts' and 'Special Entries' in the promotion stakes. In due course, this scheme became the Upper Yardman scheme, which produced about 5 per cent of the career officers in the Royal Navy in the second half of the century. Quite a few achieved Flag rank, particularly in the second half of the century.

SL transfer (transfer from the Supplementary List to the General List)

Officers of all the above forms of entry could expect a full career in the Royal Navy; from 1956 onwards, career officers, from whatever entry, were known as General List (GL) officers. Promotion was automatic up to the rank of Lieutenant-Commander, unless one was removed for misconduct, or quietly eased out for incompetence. The initial selection system ensured that there were not very many of the latter. From Lieutenant-Commander upwards, promotion was by selection. A set proportion of Lieutenant-Commanders could be expected to be selected for promotion to Commander, and so on up the chain. These proportions were not set in concrete, but were not widely varied, because it was considered bad for morale to tinker about with an officer's career prospects after he had entered. From the 1960s until the restructuring of the naval officer's career pattern in 2000, there was a requirement for junior officers (up to and including Lieutenants) substantially in excess of the number needed to fulfil the requirement for Commanders at the current promotion factor (which was about 38 per cent – i.e. 38 per cent of Lieutenant-Commanders entering the seniority zone in which they would be considered for promotion could expect to be promoted to Commander). Therefore, a short service Supplementary List entry was introduced. This had lower educational requirements, and initially entrants received a five-year commission. This form of entry brought in many high-quality candidates who had been discouraged from joining for a full career because they did not wish to commit themselves until they had seen what it was like, and opportunities were made for them to transfer to the General List.

SD transfer

Another source of officers from the lower deck was the old-fashioned warrant officer, the direct descendant of the ship's standing officers of older times: during the first four decades, a few were given commissions as Lieutenants, but could rise no further. In 1946 Warrant Officers became Commissioned Officers, but still with limited promotion prospects, and in 1956, they became 'Special Duties List' officers (SD officers), again with limited, but slightly greater, promotion prospects (they could not rise beyond the rank of Commander). In general, they were older than their peers on the General List. SD officers of sufficient potential could be selected for transfer to the General List and given an opportunity to compete on more or less equal terms with the 'Darts', etc., for promotion to Commander and onwards. However, because they were substantially older than others of their same rank and seniority, their chances of achieving Flag rank were minimal, though one or two became Captains.

2 Promotion through the Ranks, and Seniority on the Active List

In the very broadest of terms, the structure of an officer's career remained unchanged throughout the century. Until about 1955 one qualified for officer training by selection after interview, preceded by a competitive exam (sometimes the other way about); from 1955 onwards by interview having achieved academic qualifications (variously O levels, GCSE, A levels or a first degree, depending on age and type of entry). After initial training, one entered on the trained officer strength as a Lieutenant at the age of 21–22; by the end of the century, with the great majority of officers having a degree, the average age had risen to 24–25.

Seniority

Seniority in one's rank counted for a good deal. In the first place, it established one's place in the pecking order of one's peers in the same rank. This was normally of no great moment, but taking the example of two young Lieutenants, each commanding a destroyer, the senior, even by one day, would take charge as of right if they were working together. If they were of the same seniority, then the one whose name appeared first in the *Navy List* was deemed the senior; their relative position had been established by their exam results at Dartmouth and their achievements on their courses for Lieutenant.

Cadets and Midshipmen went to sea in batches from the *Britannia* or Dartmouth, and mostly their seniorities were round about the middle of January, May or September, but after the First World War round about the beginning of those months. By the time they came to be promoted to Lieutenant, the batches would have become mixed up, and depending on their course results the seniority list of Lieutenants was more or less continuous from January to December.

When it came to selection for Commander and Captain, seniority was only one of the factors taken into account; it counted for more in the first half of the century than in the second. Throughout the century, promotions to Commander and Captain were made at six-monthly intervals, again in batches; out of any one batch, the senior would have been the most senior in the rank from which they had been promoted. This tended to mean that the most junior officers in a batch were likely to be the brightest – they had attracted the attention of their senior officer after, say, only eight years as a Lieutenant, whereas the senior members of their batch of commanders had served twelve to fifteen years before their name 'came out of the hat'. When the next step in promotion came, the junior Commander in any batch might achieve promotion to Captain before his senior in his batch of Commanders. Thus, by the time a group of Lieutenants had reached the rank of Captain, their seniorities as Captain would be spread out.

To give an example, taken at random from the *Navy List*:

Captains – Seniority 30 June 1910
Senior Captain in the batch: Maurice Fitzmaurice – seniority as
    Lieutenant 14 May 1892
Junior Captain in the batch: John Dumaresq – seniority as
    Lieutenant 28 August 1894

Captains – Seniority 31 December 1910
Senior Captain: William Church – seniority as Lieutenant
    1 January 1891

Thus it will be seen that both Fitzmaurice and Dumaresq had overtaken Church in the 'promotion stakes'.

As stated above, seniority was only one factor in one's selection for higher rank. It certainly counted for more at the start of the century, but as shown above merit did bring its reward. So, too, it must be said, could nepotism and favouritism. By tradition, a Commander-in-Chief was able to nominate a promotion when he hauled down his flag. Not infrequently, his Flag Lieutenant was given the promotion, and there was at least one instance among the officers who were on the Flag List in the early years of the century where that Flag Lieutenant was a close relative. But equally, distinguished service at sea or in the field (and the Royal Navy spent a lot of time 'in the field', literally, between 1860 and 1914) could bring instant promotion – Admiral of the Fleet Earl Beatty was one who earned such a promotion, twice; to Commander, and then to Captain. He served only six years as a lieutenant (the average was ten to twelve years) before earning promotion to Commander during the Sudan campaign of 1898, and then achieved promotion to Captain, after two years as a Commander (the average was five to six years) for his actions ashore during the Boxer rebellion in China in 1900.

By the end of the twentieth century the promotion system had been refined, and officers coming up for promotion to Commander or Captain

Seaforth Publishing
FREEPOST SF5
47 Church Street
BARNSLEY
South Yorkshire
S70 2BR

DISCOVER MORE ABOUT MARITIME HISTORY

Seaforth Publishing is a maritime imprint of Pen & Sword Books, which has over 1500 titles in print covering all aspects of military history on land, sea and air. If you would like to receive more information and special offers on your preferred interests from time to time, along with our standard catalogue, please indicate your areas of interest below and return this card (no stamp required in the UK). Alternatively, register online at www.seaforthpublishing.com. Thank you.

PLEASE NOTE: We do not sell data information to any third party companies.

Mr/Mrs/Ms/Other............... Name...

Address...

.... Postcode.............

Email address...

If you wish to receive our email newsletter, please tick here ❑

PLEASE SELECT YOUR AREAS OF INTEREST

Naval - The Wooden Walls	❑	The Merchant Marine	❑		
Naval - Iron & Steel Navies	❑	Ship Modelling	❑		
Sail & Traditional Craft	❑	General Maritime	❑	ALL	❑

Website: www.seaforthpublishing.com • Email: info@seaforthpublishing.com
Telephone: 01226 734555 • Fax: 01226 734438

entered a zone for promotion, from, say, three years' seniority in the lower rank to eight years. As each six-monthly batch proceeded through the zone, it was allowed a certain quota of promotions every six months. If an officer passed though the zone without attracting the selectors' eye, then he was 'passed over'.

The Fisher-Selborne Scheme

In 1903 Admiral Sir John Fisher, then Second Sea Lord, pushed through a scheme which involved a major change to a naval officer's training and career pattern. In outline he proposed to lengthen and broaden the basic training and education, formerly given in the old training ship *Britannia*, and at the same time to introduce common training for seaman, engineer and Royal Marine officers, who would remain, broadly speaking, inter-changeable, with, for example, engineering being regarded as the equivalent of specializing in gunnery. The end result would have been a system not unlike that which the United States Navy has, or had, by which a young lieutenant may be a weapons officer in one posting, and in charge of an engine-room department in the next.

The first half of the scheme endured for over half a century, until the mid 1950s; there were additions (e.g. the 'Special Entry' scheme, and the 'Mate' scheme – see note 1 above, Form of Entry), but the second part was modified before 1912, and the altered scheme was radically modified again in the 1920s.

The first of the officers to have gone through the scheme joined the fleet as Midshipmen in 1907. The Royal Marines quickly pulled out, but the first Lieutenants (E) appeared in 1912, and until the early 1920s Lieutenants (E) appeared in the *Navy List* as 'just another specialization' – they appeared among all the Lieutenants, intermingled with (G)s, (T)s and (N)s. In the lists of ship's officers, they are included among the Lieutenants, and are 'above the salt', whereas their opposite numbers, the Engineer Lieutenants (whom they relieved on watch in charge of the engine room) were 'below the salt'. In theory, by 1940 there might have been Captains in command of major warships or flotillas who had been (E) officers. But in 1925 there occurred what very elderly Engineer Officers at the end of the twentieth century would still speak of 'the Great Betrayal'. The Board of Admiralty decided that (E) officers should be limited to a career in Engineering, and would not have command opportunities, other than of one or two specialized shore establishments. (Though there were two who had achieved command of submarines during the First World War.)

Thus by 1930 the only remaining feature of the second part of the Fisher-Selborne scheme was that all career naval officers, whether destined for the Executive, Engineer, or Paymaster Branch, did their basic education and sea training together at Dartmouth, in the Training Cruiser, and briefly in ships of the fleet as Midshipmen. And this, with the four-year education programme, remained the norm until the early 1950s.

Until the late 1960s a young officer went to sea for training as a Midshipman after completing his academic training, and basic theoretical and limited practical seamanship training. At the start of the century, he would have been about 15 years old, and would spend four years as a Midshipman, very largely in battleships. (If the vagaries of age and *Britannia* terms sent him to sea at the age of 14¾, he spent the months until he was 15 as a Naval Cadet, differentiated by his collar badge being only a twist of white braid and a button, instead of the Midshipman's white collar patch, with the twist and button superimposed.) By 1910, with the Fisher-Selborne scheme in full swing, Midshipmen went to sea at about 16½, but their time at sea as Midshipmen was reduced, until in the mid 1920s it was only two years and four months. From about 1935 onwards, the age on going to sea had risen to 17½, and time as a Midshipman reduced to twenty months: by the 1950s, it was only sixteen months.

At the start of the century, one remained a Lieutenant until one was selected for promotion to Commander. The average age for promotion to Commander was 35–38. Selection was based on reports from one's Commanding Officer, which were filtered through the Flag Officer and Commander-in-Chief in whose squadron or fleet one's ship was serving. On 1 April 1914, at the instigation of Winston Churchill, then First Lord of the Admiralty, the rank of Lieutenant-Commander was introduced to equate to the Army rank of Major. All Lieutenants, on reaching eight years' seniority as a Lieutenant, became Lieutenant-Commanders automatically: there was no further qualification needed. As a result, officers with more than eight years' seniority on 1 April 1914 were promoted immediately to Lieutenant-Commander, with a seniority date of eight years after their seniority date as Lieutenants. One result of this is of some officers having seniority as a Lieutenant-Commander apparently before the rank was introduced.

The rank insignia of a Lieutenant-Commander was two half-inch thick gold lace stripes with a quarter-inch stripe in between – hence the unofficial title of a 'two-and-a-half striper', or merely a 'two-and-a-half'. These stripes were, in fact, not new: Lieutenants of more than eight years' seniority had worn them since the 1890s. And a Lieutenant who was in command of a small craft, a sloop or destroyer, might be marked in the *Navy List* as Lieutenant and Commander, or he might sign official letters as 'Lieutenant in Command': these usages should not be confused with the rank of Lieutenant-Commander. (Furthermore, back in the mid 1850s *The Times* newspaper, in reporting naval appointments, used the phrase 'Lieutenant Commander' for Lieutenants in Command.)

Until 1918 Executive (Seaman) officers had a small curl of half-inch lace incorporated in the topmost stripe, whatever their rank. Engineer and Paymaster Officers (later Supply and Secretariat Officers) had coloured cloth between their stripes to indicate their branch, but no 'executive curl'. From 1918, all officers' stripes acquired the curl, while the distinguishing cloth remained until the provisions of Admiralty Fleet Order 1/56 came into force. Some of the colours were: Engineers (Mechanical Engineers after 1946): purple – hence 'the purple empire' for Engineers in general; Paymasters/Supply and Secretariat: white – hence 'the white mafia' for 'pussers' in general; and Electrical branch/Weapons Engineers: green – hence 'greenies'. All the above terms remained in informal general use at the end of the century (although the introduction of the centralized Ministry of Defence organization in 1964, and its increasing influence during the remainder of the century, resulted in its organization sometimes being referred to as 'the purple empire', as in 'I'm going to a purple appointment in the MoD', from the supposed result of mixing Navy Blue, Scarlet, and RAF Blue).

Throughout the century many Executive Lieutenants specialized in particular skills: Gunnery (G); Torpedo (T); Navigation (N); Signals (S), later (C) for Communications; PT (Physical Training – the 'Springers'); A/S (Anti-Submarine – this combined with the 'T' branch in 1947 to create the Torpedo Anti-Submarine Branch (TAS)). Alternatively, one could become a Hydrographic Surveyor (H), a Submariner (SM), or a Pilot (P) or Observer (O). Submariners and Aviators trained in their branch as soon as they had gained a Bridge Watchkeeping Certificate (BWK) – many submariners trained as submariners before gaining their BWK Certificate. Mostly, Executive Officers volunteered for the specialization of their choice (a few were 'pressed men'), and were sent to undertake a 'Long Course' at about the age of 25–26: one did not have to specialize, though until 1939 it was generally accepted that only those who did specialize were likely to reach the top-most ranks of the Flag List. Those who did not specialize were known as 'Salt-Horses'. The Gunnery Officer was universally known as

'Guns'; the Torpedo Officer as 'Torps', later 'Tazz'; the Navigating Officer, 'Pilot'; and the Signals/Communications Officer, 'Flags' (also used for the Flag Lieutenant, if a Flag Officer were on board). The PT officer was known as 'Bunjie', or 'the india-rubber man' (from his supposed agility as a contortionist).

From 1971 onwards, the specializations were revised, although this proved to be something of a reinventing the wheel exercise. Initially, the training of (G), (TAS), (N), and (C) officers ceased, and all 'specialists' were trained as Principal Warfare Officers (PWOs or 'Peewoes'), who were competent to operate all weapons systems. However, before very long it became necessary to subdivide PWOs into: PWO(A) – Above Water Warfare (the old (G), modernized to use missiles as well as guns); PWO(U) – Under Water Warfare (the old (TAS)); PWO(N) – the old (N); and PWO(C) – the old Communications Officer.

A specialist tended to fill only specialist appointments throughout his time as a Lieutenant or Lieutenant-Commander. 'Salt-Horses' were envied because they tended to get command at a much younger age, while still only a senior Lieutenant. However, once promoted to Commander, most Executive Officers in sea appointments were appointed regardless of their specialization. Ashore, they might fill senior specialist posts in their alma mater(s) (for example, *Excellent* or *Cambridge* for Gunnery Officers, *Vernon* or *Defiance* for Torpedo Officers), or in an appropriate staff division in the Admiralty. There were few specialist appointments for Captains, and virtually none for Flag Officers (the latter usually only in wartime). The Hydrographic Surveying specialization was effectively a navy within the Navy. Once you started at the bottom of that particular ladder, you rarely did anything else: very few Surveyors 'escaped' back to the mainstream of the 'war-fighting navy', except, perhaps, for the odd administrative appointment as, say, the Executive Officer of a shore establishment.

If one was not selected for promotion to Commander, then one was placed on the Retired List (or could apply to be placed on the Retired List) not later than the age of 45 (though this age rose to 50 in the latter half of the century). By the second half of the century everyone who had served more than a certain minimum length of time received Retired Pay while on the Retired List, the equivalent of a company pension scheme. (Although never formally stated, pay levels were set taking into account the fact that an officer apparently received a non-contributory pension – i.e. he received less pay than he would have done had his position not been pensionable.)

The rank of Commander marked a step to the Navy's higher

management. After a certain period, one became eligible for promotion to Captain, and one underwent a similar process to that undergone before one became a Commander. The rules varied over the years, and from branch to branch, but in the 1960s, the 'zone' for promotion to Commander in the Executive Branch was from three to nine years' seniority as a Lieutenant-Commander. High-fliers, potential First Sea Lords twenty-five years hence, would be picked out by the time they entered the zone, and would be promoted early to ensure that they could gain a sufficient breadth of experience before reaching Flag rank at a reasonably early age – in the case of a future First Sea Lord, before the age of 50.

For promotion to Captain, the zone in the Executive Branch in the 1960s was from four to eight years' seniority as a Commander, with an average age of promotion to Captain of 41–43. Other branches tended to promote slightly later. Those Commanders not promoted by the time they reached the top of the zone were retired compulsorily at the age of 50, later increased to 53.

Throughout the century (or until the very late 1990s), selections for promotion to Commander and Captain were announced on 30 June and 31 December annually. These fixed dates were introduced in 1885. There were exceptions – a few promotions were made for meritorious service – a seniority other than 30 June or 31 December (1 January if 31 December happened to fall on a Sunday) is an indication. From June 1956 onwards, in accordance with paragraph 50 of AFO 1/56, promotions were announced six months in advance, so the promotions for the following June were announced in December, etc. Before 1956, with the names of promotees unknown, 1 January and 1 July saw pandemonium in the offices of the Naval Secretary's appointers, since the newly promoted had to be removed swiftly to fill appointments in their new, higher rank, while some other poor wight got a 'pier-head jump' to replace them. With six months' notice given, both appointers and newly-promoted had a chance to sort things out in an orderly fashion. At the very end of the century, promotions were announced annually, up to a year in advance.

Promotion to Flag rank was treated similarly as regards selection, but Flag Officers were, at the beginning and end of the century, promoted as vacancies occurred. In between, from 1945 to 1982, promotions to Flag rank (seaman or executive branch) were made on 7/8 January and July in batches of four or so, depending on the requirement. Promotion to Flag rank in the Executive branch required that one had reached the top of the Captains' seniority list, and had had a specific amount of time in sea command, and was selected. If not, one was placed on the Retired List.

In the latter half of the century, if one had not been selected by the time one had achieved nine years' seniority, or if one reached the age of 55 before attaining nine years' seniority, one was retired.

At the turn of the nineteenth century, the rules regarding promotion to the Flag List were laid down in the 1899 edition of Queen's Regulations and Admiralty Instructions (QR.&A.I.), chapter VI, article 237, as follows (the grammar of the first clause is slightly suspect, but the meaning is clear):

> To qualify a Captain whose seniority brings him in turn for advancement to the Active list of Flag Officers, he must have completed 6 years Sea Service or its equivalent as Captain, the first three years of which must be Sea Service in command of a Ship of War at sea; or he must have completed 4 years on the books of one or more of Her Majesty's ships as a Captain during war, or 5 years of such service during war and peace combined, 3 years of such service in either case to be Sea Service in command.

> Captains who arrive at their turn for promotion without having completed the qualifying service to be retired.

Thus, provided you had completed the requisite Sea Service (see below for definitions of Sea Service), on reaching the top of the Captain's List, you were automatically promoted to Rear-Admiral. (Beatty very nearly didn't make it: because of his injuries sustained in China during the Boxer rebellion, he was unable to take up any sea appointment as a Captain for a number of years, and he reached the top of the Captain's List without having completed the requisite six years' Sea Service. A special dispensation was given to enable him to be promoted.)

Thereafter, promotion up the Flag List was purely by seniority, with the caveat that if you didn't get a Flag appointment within seven years, you would be retired on reaching the top of the relevant list.

The definition of Sea Service was laid down in Chapter V of the same edition of Q.R.&A.I. Article 213 says that Service shall mean service on full pay. Article 214 then goes on to distinguish between Harbour Service and Sea Service, mostly by defining what Harbour Service is, with everything else being Sea Service. For example, it says that 'Service in Coast Guard ships during the period of the annual cruise ... shall be reckoned as Service in a Ship of War at Sea'.

During the 1920s and 1930s, as the Navy's size decreased, there were many more Captains reaching the top of their list with all the appropriate qualifications, but for whom there were never going to be enough Flag appointments, a situation exacerbated by the financial constraints imposed during the depression of the 1930s. Thus, it became the habit to promote them to Rear-Admiral and place them on the Retired List on the same day, or the next day – much as in Nelson's day, when such Admirals became known as 'Yellow Admirals', from the non-existent squadron of which they were ostensibly to become Flag Officers. There was a substantial clear-out of the top of the Captain's List within eighteen months of the outbreak of war in 1939, although many of these retired Rear-Admirals went on to serve through the war in that rank (but on the Retired List) as Area Flag Officers, or as Convoy Commodores (as Commodores RNR).

Much the same thing occurred at the top of the Rear-Admirals' list, in the same period: a number of Rear-Admirals would come to the top of the list on, or about, the same date, and would be promoted to Vice-Admiral on the Active List for one day, and then be placed on the Retired List the next day. They would be promoted one or two at a time, so that there was never more than the officially-allowed number of Flag Officers on the Active List at any one time

Flag Officers who were employed on the Active List were placed on the Retired List automatically on reaching a certain age, which varied with rank: at the turn of the nineteenth century these were Rear-Admiral, 60; Vice-Admiral and Admiral, 65; Admiral of the Fleet, 70. For most of the century, these age limits were the same except that that for Vice-Admirals was reduced to 62. However, from 2 March 1940 onwards, Admirals of the Fleet were deemed to be on the Active List until they died. Admiral of the Fleet Sir Henry Oliver used to cite his own case as being one where the Admiralty made a bad bargain, since he lived to the age of 103. Having been promoted to Admiral of the Fleet in 1928, he was placed on the Retired List at the age of 70 in 1935, but was restored to the Active List in 1940, remaining so until his death in 1965. An officer could request that he be placed on the Retired List before the compulsory retirement age. This was sometimes done, in an era when most naval officers had private means of some sort, if an officer did not want to accept an appointment which might be uncongenial. It was also done sometimes in a genuine spirit of altruism to create a vacancy in the Flag List a year or two earlier than might otherwise have been the case, so that a younger officer could obtain his Flag, to the Navy's and his advantage.

The dates given in this section are, as stated, the officer's seniority in that rank. It is not always the date on which he first was entitled to wear the appropriate badge of rank, because there were occasions when an officer received backdated seniority on being promoted. This mostly occurred on being first promoted to Lieutenant, the rules for which remained effectively unaltered throughout the century. One could not be promoted to Lieutenant until one had gained the appropriate certificates, either on the bridge or in the engine room, but one might have gained accelerated promotion (measured in months) for achievements at varying levels on one's courses. To quote a personal example, the compiler of this record completed his Sub-Lieutenant's courses in February 1956, went to sea and gained his Bridge Watchkeeping Certificate in August 1956, and was immediately promoted to Lieutenant with seniority backdated to 1 January 1956. The amount of backdating depended on the class of pass which one gained in the exams while on course. (And one did NOT get one's pay backdated – the Treasury saw to that!)

Equally, one might have been entitled to wear badges of rank *before* the date of one's seniority. This could happen at all rank levels, if one was promoted to acting higher rank (e.g. Acting Commander) before one was promoted to the substantive post. To quote a personal example again, the compiler was selected for promotion to Commander to date 30 June 1972, but was required to fill a Commander's post before that date; so from April 1972 he was an Acting Commander, paid as a Commander, but the three months April–June did not count for seniority in that rank (nor as time for pension).

Any acting rank held by officers in the record will be recorded in the 'Rank' box alongside the appointment for which acting rank was held.

See note 11, Sources, for some notes about dates.

3 Branch

In the first half of the twentieth century, naval officers holding a commission were divided into branches and specializations. The branches were Executive (Seaman), Engineer, Paymaster (Accountant) (later Supply and Secretariat) and Instructor. To these should be added, the Air branch (from about 1938) and, from 1946, Electrical. There were sub-branches, known as specializations (rather confusing, these, since later on what had been branches became known as specializations, and what had been specializations became sub-specializations). Promotion and appointments for each branch were completely separate. It was unthinkable that a Captain (E) (for Engineer) should ever occupy a post previously occupied by a Captain (Executive, unspoken). The Executive branch filled 90 per cent (or more) of the Flag appointments. There were one or two Engineer Rear-Admirals, and usually one Engineer Vice-Admiral, but no higher rank was open to them. From 1918 onwards, Paymasters had one Flag appointment. (In excluding Medical, and later Dental, officers no slur is intended: Medical officers have always played an important part in naval life, and could be found in relatively small ships (Dental officers were rarely found in anything smaller than a cruiser), but their duties were exclusively concerned with the health of the crew rather than the working of the ship – though that point may be considered debatable, since the one can impinge on the other, and there are a number of recorded instances of Medical Officers holding Bridge Watchkeeping Certificates – strictly not in accordance with the Geneva Convention.)

Thus, the branches appear as follows:

a. **Executive**: the old 'seaman' branch – Nelson's successors, for want of a better expression.

b. **Engineering**: the old marine engineering branch; it took a long time to die, though no more new Engineers entered (other than by promotion from the lower deck, from the ranks of the artificers) after 1903.

c. **(E)**: the new Engineering branch, the result of the Fisher-Selborne scheme, as modified by the 'Great Betrayal' of 1925.

d. **Paymaster**: the branch remained (and to a great extent remains) unchanged for all practical purposes; however, in 1944 it changed its name to Supply and Secretariat.

e. **(S)**: the new Supply and Secretariat branch.

f. **Instructor**: the Instructor branch; always a very small branch.

g. **(L)**: the Electrical Branch had been formed in 1946, to be, in effect, the equivalent of the (E) branch for electrical power as opposed to mechanical power. Its members were drawn from former (T) specialists of the Executive branch, and officers who had entered via the RNVR during the Second World War.

h. **Air:** this branch was created to man the Fleet Air Arm in the run up to the Second World War. Its members were employed solely on flying duties, and could not be promoted beyond the rank of Commander.

All the above branches disappeared on 31 December 1956, as a result of Admiralty Fleet Order (AFO) 1/56. All career naval officers became members of a specialization of the General List, and the specializations appear as **X, E, L, S, I.** The Air Branch became part of the Supplementary List, and lost the suffix (A) to their rank.

Thus, officers whose career crossed the 31 December 1956 threshold will appear as, e.g.

Seaman: X or **(E): E** or **Paymaster: (S): S** – for someone who was a Paymaster prior to 1944, became a (S) officer, and in 1957 became a General List (S) officer.

Prior to 1905, officers of the Engineering branch had un-military titles, as did the Paymaster and Medical branches: a Sub-Lieutenant was an Assistant Engineer, or Assistant Paymaster, or an Assistant Surgeon; the Lieutenant equivalent was an Engineer/Chief Engineer, Paymaster or Surgeon; the Lieutenant (over eight years – later Lieutenant-Commander) equivalent was a Staff Engineer, etc.; the Commander was a Fleet Engineer, etc.; the Captain was an Inspector of Machinery, and the Rear-Admiral a Chief Inspector of Machinery. However, the Fisher-Selborne scheme of entry and training meant that future officers, whether performing executive or engineering functions would all be on a par, and so the engineering branch titles were militarized, becoming Lieutenant (E), Commander (E), etc. (new style), or Engineer Lieutenant, Engineer Commander (old style).

In 1917, in recognition of the fact that their duties in wartime were unequivocally military, the 'other' branches (other than the Executive branch, that is) were granted the right to wear the 'executive curl' on their distinction lace, and the titles of the Paymaster and Medical branches were militarized, as the engineers had been some ten years previously. So the Paymaster became the Paymaster Lieutenant; the Staff Surgeon became the Surgeon Lieutenant-Commander, etc.

Thus from the 1920s onwards engineer officers might be e.g. an Engineer Lieutenant (the old breed) or Lieutenant (E) (the new breed). By 1938, there were no more Engineer Lieutenants left on the Active List, and only two Engineer Lieutenant-Commanders (the last one left had a seniority of 1 January 1934 – he almost certainly started out as an artificer). The senior (E) officer was a Captain (E), the most senior of whom had reached the rank on 30 June 1936. The old Engineer Captains outnumbered the new Captains (E) in the proportion 39:8; at Commander level, the proportion Engineer:(E) was 75:134. On the Flag List, all eleven officers (one Vice-Admiral and ten Rear-Admirals) were Engineers. The first Rear-Admiral (E) did not arrive until 1942.

In the Rank Detail table, the ranks and seniority given are the basic military rank: under 'Rank', the rank is given as appropriate 'Engineer Lieutenant-Commander' or Lieutenant-Commander (E). Similar rules apply to the other branches. However, in anticipation of AFO 1/56, it was ordered that the various suffixes should be dropped as from 1 April *1955*.

From 1957 onwards, all career naval officers were placed on a General List, and the previous branches became known as specializations, while the specializations became sub-specializations. The intention was to open up the higher ranks of the navy to all officers whatever their specialization (X – for seaman, formerly executive; E – for Engineer (subdivided into Mechanical Engineers, ME; Weapons Engineers, WE – formed by combining the Electrical branch (L) and Ordnance Engineers (OE); S – for Supply and Secretariat; and I – for Instructor). In the last forty years of the century this has gradually happened: former (E) and (S) officers have reached the rank of Admiral, and occupied the position of Second Sea Lord. However, the X specialization retained its hold on all operational appointments, from command of any seagoing vessel up to First Sea Lord. Below the rank of Captain, most appointments are specified as being for an officer of a particular specialization, but from Captain upwards, most of the general administrative posts are open to officers of any specialization, which includes command of any major shore establishment.

In the record, officers who joined prior to 1957 are marked as being a member of the old branch structure; it may be assumed that they automatically transferred to the new specialist structure in 1956, and they are marked as shown above. Officers who joined from 1957 onwards are marked as specialists from the start.

By the end of the century, the Instructor sub-specialization had been subsumed into either the Seaman specialization (for the Meteorologists) or the E sub-specialization for the training specialists (E TM). The old (S) sub-specialist is now (2013) a Logistics branch officer.

4 Specialization/Sub-specialization

At the start of the century there were effectively only three specializations: (G) (Gunnery), (T) (Torpedo) and (N) (Navigating) in the Seaman branch. The first two specializations were the weapons technicians, dealing with all aspects of the maintenance and operations of guns, and torpedoes and mines. The (T) specialization also dealt with all matters electrical, and continued to do so up to the end of the Second World War. The (N) specialization had succeeded the old Masters and Navigating branch, which latter had been allowed to wither from 1876 onwards: one or two officers in this biography will be found to have entered the Navigating branch in the 1870s, but transferred before reaching the rank of Navigating Lieutenant.

To qualify as a specialist, an officer completed a 'Long Course', which lasted from a year to fifteen months. He usually was sent to do such a course at the age of 25 or so, when he had about three years' seniority as a Lieutenant. Thereafter, he could expect to receive a series of appointments in his own specialization, some afloat, some on a staff ashore (e.g. teaching at the parent establishment of his branch). He might do a further specialist course, going more deeply into his chosen field, and would then be marked in the *Navy List* with a 'dagger' (†), and would be known colloquially as a 'dagger G', or whatever was appropriate. Such specialists tended to go to research and development appointments, out of the mainstream of promotion.

For the first sixty years or so of the century, an officer's specialization was recognized in the *Navy List* in two places: in the seniority list, where it appeared against the names of Lieutenants, Lieutenant-Commanders and Commanders who had completed the appropriate long course, and in the list of a ship's officers, where the appropriate specialization was marked against an officer's name if he was filling a specialist billet in that ship; i.e. (G) appears against the name of a qualified (G) officer, filling the billet of Gunnery Officer in the ship. However, a (G) officer *not* filling a (G) appointment in a ship – as Staff Officer (Operations) perhaps, or as Executive Officer or First Lieutenant, would not have the (G) against his name in the list of ship's officers, though it would still be there in the seniority list. And in smaller ships, not complemented for a specialist officer, there was no indication of who did what duties – i.e. a destroyer would have an unqualified 'Gunnery Officer', but there would be no indication in the list of officers of who it was. And Captains were no longer marked with their specializations in the seniority list. In the last half of the nineteenth century (and of course, many entries in these biographies were serving in that period), the notation for the specialist varied. Initially, there was no notation, then in 1876 the use of the † symbol appeared for Gunnery Officers (then the only specialists), and later (G) and (T) appeared by 1885.

On being promoted to Commander, a specialist officer would expect to receive fewer specialist appointments, while at Captain's level there were only appointments to command his own school, or to a Director's appointment in the appropriate Admiralty/Ministry of Defence directorate. In general, it may be said that, until about 1972, the Captains of the specialist schools were always of their appropriate specialization, as were the Executive Officers

During the century, the number of sub-specializations increased: before the First World War the Signals specialist was added, denoted by the letter 'S'; from 1943 onwards, he became (C) (Communications, embracing both visual signalling – flags and lights – and radio). This may be found confusing, because 'S' was also used as an occasional abbreviation for 'Submarine', e.g. a Captain (S) was a Captain of a Submarine Section or Flotilla, analogous to a Captain (D) in a Destroyer Squadron, while the head of the submarine branch was the Rear-Admiral (S) – RA(S) – who later became FOSM (Flag Officer Submarines). For about fifty years (c.1910–1960), there was a separate PT (Physical Training) sub-specialization. Qualified submariners, indicated by the letters SM against their name in the seniority list, became a recognized sub-specialization from 1912 onwards. After the First World War, and the formation of the Royal Air Force, officers qualified for flying duties were either Pilots (P) or Observers (O). In the 1930s a few officers formed a small Anti-Submarine (AS) branch. At the end of the Second World War, the radar specialist appeared as the D (for (Fighter) Direction), and the T became the TAS with the merging of the Torpedo and Anti-Submarine branches. Finally, in the 1950s the Clearance Diver (CD) appeared, who was later extended to become the Mine warfare and Clearance Diving (MCD) sub-specialist. Another specialization was that of the Hydrographic Surveyor (H), or (H CH) – H Charge: an officer qualified to take total charge of a survey. All the above were until 1956 specializations of the Executive Branch; after 1956, they became sub-specializations of the Seaman Specialist of the General List.

The Engineering branch also was subdivided; first the Ordnance Engineer (OE) appeared, and later the Aircraft Engineer (AE). After 1956, and the combination of the Engineering and Electrical branches, the new Engineering specialization had many sub-specializations:

(E)(ME) – the Marine Engineering Specialist – the man who made the ship go! (formerly (E));

(E)(AE) – the Air Engineering Specialist – the man who made the aeroplane fly (formerly (AE));

(E)(WE) – the Weapons Engineering Specialist – the man who made the gun fire or the missile fly (formerly (L) or (OE));

(E)(MESM) – the Submarine Marine Engineering Specialist (the man who made the submarine go) – and his counterpart;

(E)(WESM) – responsible for the submarine's weapons' systems, from torpedoes to ballistic missiles.

And even this is simplifying matters.

Prior to the introduction of the (OE) and (L) branches, the (G), (TAS) and (C) officers were responsible for the maintenance and technical aspects of their respective weapons or communications systems. But the introduction of the (WE) specialization saw those responsibilities shifted to the new (WE) officer, and there was no need for the Seaman sub-specialist to have an in-depth knowledge of his equipment: he became purely an operator, a tactician. The various Long Courses, from 1960 onwards, were shortened in length (from about fifteen months to one year) as their deep technical content was removed. The new sub-specialist knew *how* his equipment worked, and *why* it worked, but he no longer knew every capacitor in the circuit, or every valve in the hydraulic system.

In the late 1960s, at the instigation of seagoing officers, a working party was set up to determine how best ships might be fought in the era of missiles, instant communications and long-range detection of the enemy. Previously, when a threat appeared there was usually time to send the ship to Action Stations, and for the '1st XI' to take charge of all their parts of the ship's weapon systems. Among the working party's conclusions was a recommendation that the sub-specialist (G, TAS, etc.) was inadequately trained for his watchkeeping duties as an Operations Room Officer: there was no longer time to close up at Action Stations when a threat was detected. The Operations Room Officer on watch, be he (G), (TAS), (D) or (C), had to be competent to engage the enemy with any or all of the ship's weapons systems. And so the old sub-specializations were abolished, and in their place there appeared the all-purpose Principal Warfare Officer (PWO, spoken as PeeWo). His knowledge of the 'guts' of his equipment was even less than his immediate predecessors, but he was, in every sense, a jack of all trades – and he was certainly master of none.

This was a misguided step. During the Second World War, most ships were organized so that when at Defence Stations (the normal wartime state, one less than Action Stations), there was a Principal Control Officer, who had the Captain's authority to engage any threat without reference to the Captain. And similarly, most Captains in the post-war years, even if they didn't give the Operations Room Officer similar authority (it was peacetime, after all) ensured that all those officers could engage the enemy with any appropriate system. And to this end, in the late 1960s all the Long Courses contained a module of cross-training in the other sub-specializations. But before these cross-trained officers had been proved at sea the PWO was introduced.

It soon became obvious that the new PWO, whose training, intended to cover the tactics and operations previously the province of four separate sub-specializations, had been shortened enormously – from one year to learn about one specialization to six months to learn about them all. As a result, before the 1970s were out, the wheel had been reinvented, and the PWO(A) (for Above-water Warfare, combining the (G) and the (D)); the PWO(U) (Underwater Warfare, formerly (TAS)); PWO(N) (the Navigation specialist) and the PWO(C) (Communications, which subsumed the increasingly important Electronic Warfare aspect) all appeared.

As a result, the situation at the end of the century in the executive branch/seaman specialization is not so widely different from that at the start of the century. Whatever his (and now one must add, or her) title, there is still a 'fighting' officer responsible for each of the ship's weapons systems.

5 Half Pay and Retirement

A commissioned officer was either on the Active List or the Retired List. Until 1938, if on the Active List, a Flag Officer was either on full pay if holding a specific appointment, or half pay if not holding an appointment (but see the paragraph below headed 'Admiralty appointments' for members of the Board of Admiralty). The same had applied to junior officers in the years leading up to the First World War, but in the years between the wars the Admiralty was more generous to officers of Lieutenant-Commander's rank and below, who were paid fully whether or not there was an appointment for them (and as junior officers there were very few for whom there was not a job); for Commanders and Captains there was limited 'unemployed pay', which gave one the basic pay for the rank without any allowances for a limited period before one was placed on half pay.

From August 1938 onwards, half pay was abolished (with the exceptions noted below) and all officers were paid the pay for their rank and seniority, regardless of whether they were in an appointment or not. They remained on full pay until they reached the retiring age for their rank.

An officer could request to be placed on the Retired List; or he was placed on the Retired List, having reached a certain age; or if, in a given rank, he had not been employed for a specific length of time.

From 1940 onwards, when Admirals of the Fleet (retired) were restored to the Active List, they received half pay, rather than retired pay, and that remains the case. Half pay remains (2013) a disciplinary sanction, for officers who have been dismissed their ship, until they are re-appointed.

Admiralty appointments

Until 1938 officers holding a commission as a Lord Commissioner of the Admiralty were paid half pay, plus a salary. The same thing applied prior to the First World War to officers holding other Admiralty appointments, such as the Director of Mobilisation, the Hydrographer of the Navy and the Director of Naval Intelligence. After the creation of the Naval Staff in 1912, naval officers on the staff were appointed to HMS *President*, the RNR drill ship in London 'for duty inside the Admiralty as Director of (e.g.) Trade Division', and were paid the naval pay of their rank. This remained the case for some sixty years, until about 1971/2, when the introduction of centralised pay accounting made HMS *Centurion*, a shore establishment at Gosport where all naval pay accounts were kept, the 'ship' to which officers serving in the Ministry of Defence (Navy) (as the Admiralty had become) were appointed.

6 Promotion on the Retired List

At the beginning of the twentieth century, Admirals of the differing grades were placed on the Retired List when they reached a certain age, or if a specified number of years had passed since they were last employed. The age limits were as follows:

Admirals of the Fleet	70
Admirals and Vice-Admirals	65
Rear-Admirals	60

However, it was still possible for an officer, having completed his career on the Active List as, say, a Vice-Admiral, to be promoted on the Retired List to the rank of Admiral. However, as announced in paragraph 80 of Admiralty Fleet Order 1/56, promotion on the Retired List ceased as of 1 January 1957 for all those retiring on or after that date. Prior to that date, promotions on the Retired List were promulgated in a 'Changes on the Retired List' section right at the end of the quarterly or half-yearly *Navy List*s. After 1 January 1957 no such notifications were made, though the implication of AFO 1/56 is that officers retiring prior to that date would continue to be promoted on the Retired List.

Furthermore, officers of Captain's rank, who for whatever reason did not reach Flag rank on the Active List, could be promoted to Rear-Admiral, and onwards and upwards (but not to Admiral of the Fleet). To quote an example, in 1908 the Chief Constable of Gloucestershire was Admiral Henry Christian. (He does not appear in these lists because he did not serve on the Active List in the twentieth century.) He had become a Mate in 1847, Lieutenant in March 1849, Commander in August 1858 and Captain in March 1863. He retired in the rank of Captain in April 1870, and was then promoted to Retired Rear-Admiral, Retired Vice-Admiral and Retired Admiral in December 1878, October 1884 and July 1889.

There was a distinction between a Retired Admiral, and an Admiral (retired): the former had never been on the Active List as a Flag officer, whereas the latter had, even though it was only for one day as a Rear-Admiral who had never hoisted his flag.

This seemingly strange procedure was a hangover of the earlier part of the nineteenth century, when, having reached 'post-rank' – i.e. Captain – an officer advanced inexorably, by seniority, up the Captain's List, and then through the various grades of the Flag List, until, in theory, if he remained alive, he could become an Admiral of the Fleet. Admiral of the Fleet Sir Provo Wallis, who had been the Second Lieutenant of the *Shannon* in her action with the USS *Chesapeake* in 1813, was promoted to Commander for that action, and was 'made post' in 1819. Unlike many less lucky officers, he did gain command at sea in the lean years following the Napoleonic wars, and was promoted to Rear-Admiral in 1851 after thirty-two years on the Captain's List, at the age of 60. He even had about ten months as a Commander-in-Chief (on the southeast coast of America) in 1857. He then became Vice-Admiral in 1857, Admiral in 1863, and Admiral of the Fleet in 1877 at the age of 86. He remained on the Active List (by special dispensation) until he died, just short of his 101st birthday. By the start of the twentieth century Admirals of the Fleet retired at the age of 70.

From 1940 onwards Admirals of the Fleet were allowed to remain on the Active List until they died. With the putting into abeyance of the rank in 1997, the most recent First Sea Lord, who normally might have expected to be promoted to Admiral of the Fleet on his last day in office (as had become the practice), was placed into a special category in the *Navy List* 'Former First Sea Lord', with the additional notation '(remains on the Active List)'. A similar entry is made in respect of former Vice-Chiefs of Defence Staff

At the end of the century, retirement ages, having been adjusted under the provisions of paragraph 58 of AFO 1/56, were as follows:

Lieutenant-Commander	50
Commander	53
Captain	55 (or after nine years' service in the rank, whichever came earlier)
Rear-Admiral	60
Vice-Admiral	62
Admiral	65
Admiral of the Fleet	Not applicable, and in any case, the rank of Admiral of the Fleet had been placed in abeyance in 1997. However, former First Sea Lords, who prior to that date might have expected promotion to Admiral of the Fleet, remained on the Active List, but were placed in a separate category in the *Navy List*.

In addition to Flag Officers, officers of lower rank could be promoted on the Retired List: Lieutenants (which rank, after 1914 included Lieutenant-Commanders) and Commanders could be promoted on the Retired List to Captain, but no further (though there were a few exceptions). Similar conditions applied to Warrant Officers, who could reach the rank of Lieutenant (and later Lieutenant-Commander) on the Retired List.

Another form of promotion on the Retired List was War Service Rank (WSR). During the Second World War many retired officers were recalled for service, and served in a rank higher than that which they had held on the Active or Retired Lists. Thus an officer might have retired as a Lieutenant-Commander, been promoted to Commander on the Retired List, and served during the war in the rank of Captain. He would be entitled to call himself Captain So-and-So, and wear a Captain's uniform on appropriate occasions. In the career details of such an individual, his final rank is given as Lieutenant-Commander, but his 'on retirement' rank and name is given as Captain So-and-So.

None of these promotions made any difference to your retired pay (except a prolonged period of WSR service, which might improve your retired pay).

7 Record of Service

Dates

In this section are listed the ships in which each officer served, the date he was appointed to that ship, and the duties for which he was borne in that ship. Where the record has been compiled from his Service record, whether in the National Archives or from records still in the hands of the MoD, the date of appointment is that given in the record. The records show a date from which the officer was no longer borne on the books of his ship. If he were travelling back to the UK from a foreign station, he might have left his ship up to two months prior to the date on which he came off her books. In some cases it has been possible to determine more nearly the date on which he left the ship, because he is marked as being 'victualled only' in the ship in which he took passage home. The records also use the word 'superseded', which indicates the date on which his relief was appointed.

For officers whose personal records are not available, or incomplete, reliance has been placed on the *Navy List*. The date 'from which' appears therein and should be the date of appointment (but sometimes differs from the date in the service record). If the officer had to take passage to a foreign station, the date given is the day he joined the troopship or liner, in which he took passage out. So, for example, if joining a ship on the Australia station in the 1890s, the date of appointment of an officer was some six weeks before the date he actually arrived on board. As regards the date he left, all that can be said is that he left before the date of his appointment to his next ship. It is sometimes possible to deduce the likely date on which an officer left – the Captain and Commander were unlikely to leave without relief, and so there is an excellent chance that the date given for a relief joining will be the date on which his predecessor left. But, as explained above, where the ship was on a foreign station, the date of his successor's appointment most probably pre-dated his own leaving date by anywhere between two weeks (for the Mediterranean) to six weeks (for the stations in the Far East). All the above applied in the years before the Second World War, though the time gap had decreased to about four weeks for the Australia and China stations. And successive *Navy List*s might give different dates for an officer joining a ship. They usually differed by no more than a day or two, and might be due to the earlier one being the day an appointment was due to take effect, while the later one was the day actually reported in due course – due to circumstances beyond an officer's control. However, for the first half of the century, the *Navy List* gave the actual date of an Admiral's hoisting his flag, as well as the earlier date of appointment. So the date of appointment is just that, while the date of hoisting his flag is given in the text part of the entry, under the heading 'Appointment'.

The *Navy List*s were full of anomalies. Not all officers were appointed to a ship. At the turn of the nineteenth century, 95 per cent or so of officers in receipt of full pay were appointed to a ship, but there were exceptions: these included senior officers who were Lords Commissioners of the Admiralty; officers who were employed in the Admiralty in the Naval Intelligence Department; officers who were attachés in foreign countries; officers who had appointments under another department (e.g. serving on the Ordnance Committee, under the Master-General of the Ordnance); officers who were attending courses (the staff who taught them might be appointed to a ship, but the students weren't – but sometimes it was the other way about). See note 5, Half Pay and Retirement, under 'Admiralty appointments'.

Nor were the dates on which they took up those appointments given (except, for some reason, attachés). And records do exist (though not in the earlier twentieth-century *Navy List*s) of the dates of appointment to the Board of Admiralty – these were peculiar, in that a new Commission was made out each time any member of the Board changed, whether political or naval, so a single two-year appointment may appear as four or more separate appointments. Gradually, the system changed; with the formal establishment of a naval staff at the Admiralty in 1912, it became the general rule (but with several exceptions) that all officers serving in the Admiralty were appointed to HMS *President* (additional) and their dates of appointment were given. From the 1920s to the 1970s this rule held good – except for Lords Commissioners of the Admiralty, who were paid from a different Vote in the Naval Estimates, and so were not appointed to a ship. Between the First World War and the Second World War, two dates were frequently given: the date that the officer took up the appointment, and an earlier date – from one day to six months earlier – on which he joined the appropriate division or department. It is assumed that this was for turnover, and that the rationale for publishing both dates was that the Treasury would not allow two officers to be paid for the same appointment, unless there was a good reason! Until the late 1930s Flag Officers appointed to, for example, the Senior Officers' Technical Course, were not appointed to a ship, but officers below Flag rank, on the same course, at the same time, were. And it will be noted that there were some occasions when officers were deemed to be on full pay, even if they weren't actually filling their complement billet.

Examples are: officers appointed to ships on foreign stations, who went on to full pay when they joined the troopship or liner taking them to Hong Kong, or wherever, and some officers taking up Admiralty appointments who doubled up with their predecessors for a turnover period of a week or so (see above).

The result of all these variables is that where a full date (day, month, year) is given, it may be taken as being a date taken from his Personal Record, now held in the National Archives or by the MoD: failing those, it will have been taken from the final *Navy List* in which the officer appears in that appointment (by that time, it is to be hoped that any errors had been bowled out). Where only a month and year is given, it will be either because the full date has never been given (as with some Admiralty appointments, or particularly for periods of unemployment or half pay), or because, particularly during the First World War, the *Navy List* just did not give dates. Under those circumstances, the month given is that of the earliest *Navy List* in which the officer appears in that appointment. Dates of relief in a post, or of hauling down a flag, are given in the short text which appears with each appointment.

Officers appointed 'additional' or 'supernumerary'

Quite frequently, officers would be appointed 'additional', or 'supernumerary'. This did *not* imply that they had nothing to do, but that they were borne, over and above the established complement of the ship, for some other purpose (as it might be, for a local survey). One specific example concerns Midshipmen in the period 1875–1900: it was held that the young officers *must* be trained in sail, so they were sent in large numbers to the masted cruisers that formed the bulk of ships on foreign stations. The result was that many more Midshipmen were carried in a ship than were complemented, and a quarter of the gunroom officers might be officially supernumeraries. But as the senior batches in a ship completed their Midshipman's time and moved on, the junior batch then became part complement. In other cases it was due to the Admiralty having failed to catch up with the facts of life, and the needs of the fleet, in amending schemes of complement. As an example, in the 1870s officers qualifying as Gunnery Lieutenants were all borne 'additional' in the *Excellent*, without any indication of what they were there for. By 1885 they are still borne 'additional', but it is now specified that they were 'qualifying for Gunnery Lieutenant'. Later on, they appeared separately in the various lists of officers undergoing courses: in the alphabetical list, their 'ship' would appear as '(G) Course', while in the list of 'Officers qualifying for (G)', their name would appear, with the notation 'borne in *Excellent*'. Further examples occurred where officers were on 'detached service', but had to be borne on some ship's books; a particular example was Ascension Island (then used as a coaling station) which in the first decade of the twentieth century was run as a ship with a Captain in command. He and all the crew were appointed additional to the guard-ship at Simonstown, down at the Cape of Good Hope.

Yet another example concerns officers appointed to the Admiralty, whether for a job on the naval staff, or as a member of the Board: it was customary for them to do a turnover (reading in to the new job) for a period varying from a couple of days to four weeks (the latter for a Board appointment). They would be appointed *President*, additional during that period, then be reappointed *President* additional as Director of 'Whatever'. If they were appointed for some one-off task, then they would be appointed for 'special service'. Later on, officers appointed to an Admirals' staff would be appointed to HMS *Nonsuch* additional for the staff of CinC ...

Half pay

At the start of the twentieth century, it was still the custom that on leaving a ship an officer was placed on half pay until he was appointed to his next ship, so leave between appointments (except between long foreign appointments) was something of an expensive luxury. However, in the case of an officer leaving a ship on a foreign station, it might be as long as three months from the date of his being relieved in the ship before he was placed on half pay: his time on passage home still counted as full pay time, and foreign service leave after, say three and a half years on the China station, was one week for every six months abroad – in this case, seven weeks.

Until the abolition of half pay, officers might be appointed to serve on Admiralty and other committees while on half pay; they might also undertake various courses. For some of the latter, they might be 'properly' appointed, and paid full-pay rates – but more often they were only on half pay.

Half pay finally disappeared in 1938 (with the exception that an officer could still be placed on half pay for disciplinary reasons – a sanction which remained until the end of the century – and still remains). After the First World War, 'unemployed pay' was introduced for officers below Flag rank. Broadly speaking, an officer leaving a ship, and not immediately appointed to another, was entitled to 'unemployed pay' (which was his full rate of pay, without allowances) for up to six months, as long as he held himself 'at the disposal of the Admiralty'; after six months, or if he said, 'Please don't give me another ship for three months, I want to enjoy some hunting,' he went on to half pay – which was just that. Flag Officers were not granted this indulgence – they were either in employment on full pay, or half pay: going on a course did not count as 'being in employment' – you did the course on half pay

So long as the *Navy List* was produced at intervals of no more than three months, it will produce a virtually complete record of an officer's service, but there might be occasions when an officer was appointed to a ship, but before his name could appear in the *Navy List*, circumstances had altered – he might have been appointed to another ship, consequent upon, say, an accident, or his first ship might have been sunk. In the higher ranks, an officer 'between appointments' might be employed in carrying out a short study, or some other similar job, or sent on a course: these quite frequently did not appear in the *Navy List*.

Ships, their types, and where they were stationed

In the case of most officers who completed a full career, their first 'ship' was the training ship or shore establishment, situated at Dartmouth since 1863. Until 1905 it was the succession of old 'wooden walls' which were known collectively as HMS *Britannia*. From 1905 the two colleges (the junior at Osborne – actually opened in 1903 – and the senior at Dartmouth) were usually known as RNC (Royal Naval College) Osborne or Dartmouth, though members of the staff were borne on the books of a name ship. These were (Osborne) *Racer* and *Osborne*, and (Dartmouth) *Espiegle* and (from 1910) *Pomone*. In 1922, Osborne having closed two years earlier, the College at Dartmouth again became HMS *Britannia*, and remained so until the new royal yacht was launched in 1952. It then became the 'Britannia Royal Naval College, Dartmouth', usually shortened to BRNC. (The college also had a name ship as HMS *Dartmouth* though this was rarely used.)

The other major form of officer entry was the Special Entry. From the scheme's inception in 1913 until the outbreak of war in 1939, their initial training was quite separate, and was based in various demilitarised ships at Devonport (during the First World War, ashore at Devonport). From 1939 onwards their training was carried out under the same roof as *Britannia*/BRNC (though separately from the younger entries) until the scheme ended in 1955.

In our officers' records we have used *Britannia* for those who entered under the old scheme; *RNC Osborne & Dartmouth* for those who entered 1903–1922 under the Fisher-Selborne scheme; *Britannia*, 1922–1952; and BRNC thereafter. For Special Entries, we have used the name of the current ship in use until 1939, thereafter *Britannia*/BRNC as appropriate.

From an officer's first going to sea, he was appointed to a series of ships. A brief description of the ship has been included in most cases – usually the description given in the *Navy List*. These varied over the years, thus, in the earliest entries, from the late 1850s and early 1860s, a ship may be described as a 'screw steam frigate'; from 1861, the word 'steam' is omitted. And a ship, which in the 1870s might be described as a 'screw sloop', became, in the 1890s, a '3rd class cruiser', and so on. The description used is that given in the *Navy List* of the date of the officer's appointment. And up until the First World War, the *Navy List* gave an indication, with the list of officers, of where the ship was employed; however, after 1914 this ceased, although until the Second World War the information was available elsewhere in the *Navy List*.

Until 1913 ships continued to have the number of guns they carried as part of their 'title' in the *Navy List*. This was a hangover of the days when ships were 'rated' according to the number of guns they carried. Thus the old *Dreadnought* of 1872 appears as *Dreadnought*, 4 – she had four 12.5in guns in two turrets (plus half a dozen smaller guns which weren't counted), while her successor, Jackie Fisher's *Dreadnought* of 1906 appears as *Dreadnought*, 10 – she had ten 12in guns in five turrets (plus twenty-seven 12pdrs – 3in quick-firers – they didn't count either). The battleship *Inflexible* of 1881, which Jackie Fisher commanded as a Captain, appears as *Inflexible*, 4, while her successor, one of the first battlecruisers, is *Inflexible*, 24. This was clearly illogical: it would seem that the rule was that *Dreadnought*'s secondary armament of 12pdrs wasn't counted, whereas *Inflexible*'s 4in were. The gun rating might vary over the years, too, as ships' armaments were changed; e.g. *Warrior*, 40, in 1861, had become *Warrior*, 32, by 1883. Indeed, the gun rating might vary during a commission – e.g. *Canada* was rated at 14 guns when Prince George of Wales joined her in May 1883, but she was rated '10' when he left her a year later.

The figures were totally meaningless by the start of the twentieth century, but have been included as a curiosity, and because, as stated above, they continued to be recorded in the *Navy List* until January 1913. So details of appointments prior to that date will include the figure where appropriate; thereafter they do not appear.

There were also ships which had no gun rating; the old hulks which acted as depot ships at the turn of the century were examples. But *Excellent*, while still afloat, though with many guns as befitted her status as gunnery training school, was unrated, or became so. Later though, when entirely ashore on Whale Island, she became *Excellent*, 1! There has to be a suspicion that some senior Gunnery Officer said, 'Ridiculous, you can't have the Gunnery School apparently without any guns'. And the earlier destroyers, whose largest gun was a 12pdr, had no gun rating – the 12pdr didn't count – see the comment on *Dreadnought* above. So an 1890s TBD, armed perhaps with one 12pdr and three 3pdrs (a typical armament) has no gun rating. Later on, there were 'scouts' – a very light cruiser, intended to act as the leader for destroyer flotillas – which were armed with up to ten 12pdrs, who therefore had no gun rating. But as soon as destroyers started to grow, and were armed, e.g. with a single 4in gun and a number of smaller weapons, they were given a gun rating (the 'B' class destroyers of 1909 onwards were the first entire class to be so armed and rated).

The result was that just before the outbreak of the First World War the most modern battleship in the fleet, *Iron Duke*, was officially *Iron Duke*, 22 (her ten 13.5in guns, and the twelve 6in guns of her secondary battery).

Appointment/duties

Officers in command of any of HM Ships, of whatever rank, are marked 'In command', whatever their rank might have been. On board, they would have been known as 'the captain' – regardless of the actual rank held, or less reverently as 'the old man', 'the skipper', 'the owner', or 'father'. The last was usually a wardroom expression, the others were both lower-deck and wardroom usage. A number of Captains (by rank) were appointed as Commodores, in command of a small squadron or a minor station, or as a Chief of Staff to a Flag Officer. One or two officers in command appear as Rear-Admirals. With the exception of the Flag Officer, Royal Yachts, who was also the commanding officer of whichever yacht he was in, this is because they have been promoted while in command, and remained in command for a month or so until their relief could reach the ship to take over.

The second-in-command of a cruiser or larger ship (battleship, aircraft carrier) was almost universally of Commander's rank. He was referred to as 'the Commander'. Here the expression 'the Executive Officer' has been used throughout. This phrase is of long standing and avoids the complications of a Commander who is a captain (or even, as occurred once or twice in the 1950s, of a commander who was a Captain – HMS *Eagle* briefly had an officer of Captain's rank (but a junior Captain) as Executive Officer in one commission). The Commander's nickname was 'the Bloke'. This was almost exclusively a lower-deck expression.

In a smaller ship, the second-in-command was known as 'the First Lieutenant'. He was of Lieutenant-Commander's or Lieutenant's rank, or even, in a very small ship, merely a Sub-Lieutenant. In these tables he is referred to as 'the First Lieutenant'. His nickname was 'Jimmy the One', 'James' (wardroom facetiousness), or 'the Jim'. A battleship, having a Commander as Executive Officer, would also have the senior Lieutenant-Commander or Lieutenant as the First Lieutenant. His responsibilities were then usually confined to ship's housekeeping below decks (but see below); the Commander's deputy on the upper deck was the 'Mate of the Upper Deck'.

Next came the specialists/sub-specialists (see note 4). They had their nicknames, most of them being fairly obvious: 'Guns' (and 'Little Guns', where a second qualified (G) officer was carried); 'Torps'; 'Pilot' (the Navigating Officer – sometimes known as 'Vasco' (da Gama)); 'Flags' (for the Communications Officer, even after flag signalling had dropped out of use). The term 'Flags' was always used for the Admiral's Flag Lieutenant in a flagship, and the ship's signals/communications officer would have some other name – usually just his own – but not 'bunts', a lower deck-term for a signal rating.

Other non-specialist officers are marked as 'for watchkeeping and divisional duties'. They would have had specific duties, but these were not detailed in the *Navy Lists*. In a big ship, such duties would primarily have been such positions as Officer of the Quarters in one of the main armament turrets, and being the divisional officer responsible for a section of the ship's upper deck and the seamen who worked there. These were the Foc's'le division, the Foretop, the Maintop and the Quarterdeck; in a smaller ship, the two Top divisions would have been combined, and called merely the Top; while in a destroyer, the central division was known as the Waist. In a battleship, the job of Maintop Divisional Officer would have included being Boats Officer – responsible for the half-dozen or so boats carried, which were usually stowed on the boat deck at the foot of the mainmast, while the Foretop Officer might also be the Boy Seamen's Divisional Officer. The officer responsible for the Foc's'le part of ship was also, usually, the Cable Officer – responsible for the ship's anchors and cables. But this might sometimes be the First Lieutenant's responsibility. A good captain would switch such duties round to ensure that his officers gained experience at all the jobs. It should be emphasised that 'divisional duties' took up a good portion of an officer's time: they involved being responsible for the welfare and career progression of a body of men, most of whom were responsible directly or indirectly to the divisional officer. Thus the Gunnery Officer would be responsible for the gunnery ratings, and so on.

In destroyers and frigates, it was unusual to find specialist officers: there was one of each specialization borne in the Flotilla (later in the century, Squadron) Leader, who might move around the ships of the squadron in turn, giving advice, and watching over the unqualified officers who had the appropriate responsibility in the other ships. Sometimes single ships on a detached mission might have a specialist – particularly a specialist Navigator. But in 'ordinary' destroyers the Gunnery Officer would be an officer of Lieutenant's rank, who had done a short course on the particular weapons system fitted in his ship; similarly, the Navigator would be a DNDO (Destroyer Navigation and Direction Officer – the compiler of these notes was one such, in HMS *Dunkirk*, 1958–9). The Torpedo Officer in a small ship would have been a Warrant Officer until about 1950.

During the latter half of the century, most destroyers and frigates had a specialist (G) and (TAS) officer, but specialist (N) and (C) officers were still only found in the Squadron Leader. The Sub-Lieutenant was usually made the ship's correspondence officer and ran the ship's office – and other officers had such jobs as laundry officer (scarcely a promotion job, but it did have its perks, particularly if you had a Chinese laundry crew), while at the bottom of the heap came the SLJO – sh*tty little jobs officer. In the wardroom, someone was the wine caterer – frequently, and the rule applied throughout the century, this was the Medical Officer when one was borne, on the grounds that he had little else to do. (This was not entirely unfair – young men are inherently healthy, and the doctor usually had only accidents to deal with, plus, inevitably, cases of venereal disease.)

In the Engine Room Department, the head of the department, of whatever rank, was *the* Engineer Officer, known as the 'Chief'. This was largely wardroom usage – to a rating, a chief, or the chief, was the Chief Petty Officer of his division, or branch – but it was a long recognized term, and the Captain would use the expression while on duty – e.g. when the Engineer Officer reported the machinery ready for sea, the Captain would probably reply, 'Very good – thank you, Chief.' The deputy engineer officer was 'the Senior Engineer', usually known just as 'the Senior'. As a rule, in a big ship having several watchkeeping engineers, he did not keep watches, but he was usually the damage control engineer officer.

Engineer Lieutenants' duties were similarly allocated in the larger ships, where there might have been three or four Engineer Lieutenants, or Lieutenants (E). Their primary duties were watchkeeping in the engine room, but each was given ancillary duties as well. There was the 'double bottom' officer, who looked after the stowage of fuel in the tanks in the double bottoms, and all the other compartments in the lower parts of the ship; in an aircraft carrier, the Flight Deck Engineer Officer looked after all the flight deck machinery, catapults, arrester gear and the like.

The Electrical branch barely had time to get its titles into general usage, before it became the Weapons branch, after being amalgamated with the Ordnance Engineers. However, the Electrical Officer might be addressed, off duty, as 'El-san' – a piece of small-boy humour, from the initial letter of his branch title, (L), and the mock-Chinese honorific 'san', the whole making up the name of a chemical closet.

Other names used informally were 'the Pusser', for the senior Paymaster, later Supply, officer on board, and if the Captain enjoyed the luxury of a young Paymaster/Supply officer as his Captain's Secretary, he was known as 'Scratch', and often addressed as such by the Captain. (The present branch title of 'Logistics' was introduced in the early twenty-first century.) 'Wings' was the Commander (Air) in an aircraft carrier, and his deputy, the Lieutenant-Commander (Flying) was known as 'Little F'.

In submarines, the Executive Officer was always the First Lieutenant ('the Jim'), and the remainder of the Seaman officers were the Second, Third, Fourth, and Fifth Hands. (Very much older submariners would use the expression 'second dicky' for the First Lieutenant, from the days when a submarine only had two, perhaps three, officers.) Until the advent of the nuclear submarine, it was very rare, other than during the First and Second World Wars, to find an officer of more than Lieutenant-Commander's rank in command of a submarine. But officers of Commander's and Captain's rank might be marked 'and for service with submarines', which indicated that they were entitled to receive submarine pay – which used to be a substantial enhancement to one's pay (e.g. it was 6s per diem in 1918, which was a 44 per cent increment for a Lieutenant, 26 per cent for a Commander; in 1958 it was 11s, being a 23 per cent increment for a Lieutenant, 12.5 per cent for a Commander). Nuclear submarines, whether attack submarines or ballistic missile submarines, were always Commander's commands.

The above list is not exhaustive, but covers most eventualities.

Career pattern

As a very general rule, the career pattern for executive (seaman) officers remained unchanged throughout the century, though for the second half the initial training period changed.

Midshipman: under training. At the start of the century, aged 15–19 (a few went to sea while still under 15 and were ranked as Naval Cadets). From the opening of Dartmouth in 1905 to the end of Dartmouth as a 'public school'/sixth form college (1955, when the COST scheme was introduced) the age range was 17–20. During these fifty-five years the Midshipman's training time went down from three and a half years to sixteen months. In training terms, the purpose was to train an officer in seamanship, and the completion of a Midshipman's time was marked by the passing of one's Seamanship Board, when you were examined in practical seamanship by three officers, the senior of whom would be a Captain or Commander

The compiler of these notes is of the opinion that there was no finer training than that given to Midshipmen: you might be referred to as 'the lowest form of animal life', but you were given responsibility in small things at a very early stage; you learned to handle men, usually older than yourself. If you made mistakes, the lesson might be reinforced by punishment, but it was never held against you.

Sub-Lieutenant: initially, the young officer was promoted to Acting Sub-Lieutenant, and went on a series of courses to fit him for the rank of Lieutenant. For the first half of the century this period lasted from about nine to eighteen months, and comprised a period at the Royal Naval College, Greenwich, followed by a series of professional courses at Portsmouth. At the beginning of the century the courses consisted of Gunnery, Torpedo, Navigation and Pilotage; by the mid 1950s, the Greenwich course lasted eight months, and was known as the Junior Officers' War Course, and was run along the lines of a university. The professional courses comprised Gunnery, Torpedo & Anti-Submarine, Navigation (which included practical Pilotage), Communications, Air, Damage Control, Electrical, Divisional (Administration) and Amphibious Warfare, these last nine courses lasting nine months. At the end of that time, provided all courses had been passed, you were confirmed as a Sub-Lieutenant, in 99 per cent of cases with the same seniority as on promotion to acting rank. The class of pass gained counted to allow backdated seniority in the rank of Lieutenant. It may be noted that the pass marks were high, compared to some of the grades in public examinations in 2013. Thus 84 per cent would only get you a second-class pass; a third had to be over 65 per cent

A confirmed Sub-Lieutenant was given a sea appointment to gain his Bridge Watchkeeping Certificate (BWK Cert). The award of this was entirely in the gift of one's Captain, and would usually take a minimum of six months, but this could depend on the amount of sea-time the ship did during that time.

A Sub-Lieutenant became eligible for promotion to lieutenant when he had three years' seniority as a Sub-Lieutenant, provided he had gained his BWK Cert. His seniority could be backdated by up to sixteen months if he had gained maximum seniority in all his courses. In small ships, Sub-Lieutenants messed in the wardroom with the other officers, but in cruisers, battleships and aircraft carriers carrying Midshipmen, they messed in the gunroom with other Sub-Lieutenants (Engineers and Paymasters/Supply branch). The senior Executive branch Sub-Lieutenant was *the* Sub-Lieutenant of the Gunroom, and a man of great importance in the lives of the Midshipmen.

Lieutenant: until the very end of the 1990s, one served a minimum of eight years as a Lieutenant, in an age range of 22–32. In that time you were expected to be able to fill any complement billet for an Executive Officer of that rank. You might also specialize (see note 4) during those eight years: if you became a submariner or aviator or hydrographic surveyor, then you would stay in that branch until you reached the rank of Commander, and frequently as Commander and Captain. Senior Lieutenants might command small submarines, destroyers, minesweepers. Such commands were highly prized. As a sub-specialist officer you would expect to fill a series of sub-specialist posts at sea, interspersed with training posts in your sub-specialist school, or R & D.

At the start of the century, the next rank up was Commander, achieved after eleven to eighteen years' service as a Lieutenant, but in April 1914, automatic promotion to an intermediate rank, called **Lieutenant-Commander**, was introduced. This occurred on the officer's attaining eight years' seniority as a Lieutenant. Promotion to Commander was solely by selection, and was based on the succession of reports made by your Captains. There was a zone of seniority during which one was eligible for promotion, and selections were made at six-monthly intervals. (The zone's limits varied over the years.) If you had not been promoted to Commander by the time you had reached the end of 'the zone', you were 'passed over', and could remain in the lower rank until retirement age. Lieutenant-Commanders commanded destroyers, and, if specialists, filled senior staff and training posts.

The rank of **Commander** was reached at the age of about 32–33, at the youngest, to 41–42. A late promotion was unlikely to advance further; a future First Sea Lord would have to have been an early promotion – a 'first-shot' promotion – so that he could gain sufficiently varied experience before reaching Flag rank. It marked a step-change in an officer's career: prior to this point he was almost exclusively a doer, a man of action; from here on, he was as much, if not more, a thinker, a policy maker or administrator, an overall director of units large or small, as he had previously been a comparatively small-scale man of action.

Commanders commanded small corvettes, destroyers, frigates, or were the Executive Officer (second-in-command) of cruisers, battleships and aircraft carriers. A high degree of organizational skill was required to run a battleship. With the formation of the Naval Staff from 1912 onwards, Commanders filled the duties of what were termed desk officers in the various directorates: Operations and Trade, Naval Intelligence, etc. The names have changed, and responsibilities reapportioned over the years, but the task remains the same: to determine policy and set it in train.

A similar zone system applied to promotion to Captain: again the period varied over the years, but mostly was between four and eight years. As stated above, everything depended on the reports rendered by your senior officers. So, a good relationship was essential if you wanted to achieve promotion: service in a flagship was sought after, because you came under the Admiral's personal eye (though this could be a two-edged weapon – get on the wrong side of the Admiral, and your career could be blighted).

Captain: Captain's rank would be achieved between the ages of 36 (the high-flying potential First Sea Lord) and 47–48 (David Beatty was exceptional – he became a Captain just under the age of 30). On the Captain's List seniority applied, and promotions to the Flag List were made (or not made) when you reached the top of the Captain's List. To be eligible for promotion to Flag rank, it was necessary to have had a set amount of sea-time in command, and so Captains were at pains to seek those appointments. Prior to the First World War, most Captains achieved promotion to Flag rank on the Active List, even though many never flew their flag at sea: some were promoted, and placed on the Retired List the next day. However, even if you retired as a Captain, you could still be promoted on the Retired List – there are examples of officers who retired as a Captain, but still ended up as a Retired Admiral. There was a subtle difference between a Flag Officer, retired, and a retired Flag Officer. The former had served on the Active List in Flag rank, the latter had not. Promotion on the Retired List was abolished in 1956. At the end of the century, Captains were retired if they reached nine years' seniority without being selected for the Flag List, or on reaching the age of 55, whichever was the earlier

Captains commanded ships, or flotillas/squadrons of smaller ships; after the formation of the Naval Staff from 1912 onwards, senior Captains became the Directors of Directorates or Divisions, junior Captains became Assistant Directors. Prior to 1914, shore appointments for officers were confined to the training schools (by this time, nearly all housed ashore); thereafter, the proportion of shore appointments rose steadily.

At the start of the century, promotion through the ranks of the Flag List was solely by seniority: appointments were rationed. **Rear-Admirals** had one seagoing appointment, for twelve months to the day, almost, as the second-in-command of a squadron or fleet. Thereafter, if they had done particularly well, or were very well connected, they might get a second appointment, but the majority were promoted to Vice-Admiral by seniority, and even to Admiral, without any further employment, finally being placed on the Retired List because they'd reached the age limit, or because a specified period, seven years in most cases, had elapsed since they had last had an appointment.

The period between the wars saw the rules being changed. Promotion up the Flag List depended on the requirement for Admirals, and officers were selected for promotion to Vice-Admiral and Admiral. The Naval Secretary (an officer of Rear-Admiral's rank) kept the 'flag plot', a highly-confidential document which set out the likely progression of senior Flag Officers' appointments, so that the career progression of the next-First-Sea-Lord-but-three could be followed: the parameters were largely set by the current First Sea Lord. There was usually an alternative path for a second choice, but an unexpected death or resignation could throw the whole flag plot out of kilter.

There were 'good appointments' and there were dead-end appointments. For example, before the First World War, if a Captain was coming to the top of the Captain's List, and was appointed to command of one of the port guard-ships, that was tantamount to saying that he would not get his flag on the Active List. Later on, after the Second World War, there was a pecking order in the Naval Staff Divisions – the Director of Naval Operations and Trade was a near-certainty for his flag as was the Director of Plans/Naval Plans, but the Director of one of the administrative divisions was much more likely to fail to do so.

8 Honours and Awards

At the start of the twentieth century, the system of honours and awards was, in principle, much as it was until just before the end of that century. There were honours, in the form of a number of Orders of Chivalry, with various grades, and there were awards, in the form of medals for bravery or distinguished service (not necessarily for bravery).

So far as the Royal Navy was concerned, the main honour was the Military Order of the Bath, which had then, as it still does, three grades: in rising order, Companion (CB), Knight Commander (KCB) and Knight Grand Cross (GCB). At the start of the century, meritorious service by a Captain or Rear-Admiral might be rewarded by appointment as a CB; a Vice-Admiral or Admiral could expect a 'K' (i.e. to become a Knight Commander, and with it the honorary title of 'Sir'), while only senior Admirals and Admirals of the Fleet became GCBs, which brought no other honorific. It would be rare to find a Commander receiving a CB; equally, there were few Admirals who hadn't received some honour by the time they reached that rank, though a glance at the list will show that there were some, especially in the years before the First World War. The reason, if reason be needed, for the lack of what might otherwise seem to have been an appropriate honour, is rarely known. However, until the First World War, there were a number of Vice-Admirals and Admirals on the Active List, who had not been employed since they were Rear-Admirals: they could not normally be expected to receive a senior honour. However, the author can say with certainty that there have been examples of honours being offered, but declined. Naval officers might also become members of the Civil Order of the Bath, though this was not a very frequent occurrence after the First World War.

The Order of St Michael and St George had the same grades (CMG, KCMG, and GCMG), and was primarily for diplomatic services, or for naval services in war, not involving contact with the enemy. At the end of the twentieth century, it is virtually unheard of to find a naval officer as a member of this order, but a hundred years earlier, when officers of the Royal Navy still performed a diplomatic role, particularly on the more distant stations, there were quite a few senior officers who were members of this order. It was also used to reward other meritorious services which were neither strictly naval, nor diplomatic, but which were associated with his job.

Membership of the Royal Victorian Order was in the personal gift of the sovereign, and at this time had the same grades as the other orders (CVO, KCVO, GCVO). It was usually the case that officers having membership of this order had served in one or other of the Royal Yachts, or had rendered services to a member of the royal family in some other connection, not always naval. There were also two more junior grades: MVO (4th class) (a Member), which has now become LVO (Lieutenant); and MVO (5th class – remains MVO). It has to be said that the criteria for this award seem to have varied over the century – King Edward VII seems to have handed out MVOs and CVOs like sweeties! It became the custom for the sovereign to award membership of the order, of the appropriate grade, to the Admiral commanding the fleet at a royal review – the implication was that it was recognition that the Admiral had taken care of the fleet for the monarch.

At the end of the nineteenth century, there were two other Orders, both relating to India: the Order of the Indian Empire, the junior of the two, and the Order of the Star of India. Their grades were CIE, KCIE, GCIE, and CSI, KCSI, GCSI. There were few naval members of these orders (any Flag Officer with one or other had probably been CinC East Indies or Flag Officer commanding the Royal Indian Navy).

There were also the Orders of Knighthood: the Garter (KG), the Thistle (KT), and St Patrick (KP). The latter two orders are reserved for Scotsmen or Irishmen for exceptional services in those countries (and are rare at the end of the twentieth century, KPs in particular), while the Garter is a national order for the United Kingdom as a whole. There remained also the Hanoverian Order, but this had ceased to be awarded by the British crown when Queen Victoria came to the throne, and Hanover reverted to its own king; none of our subjects were members of this order, though their seniors when they joined, might have been. And there was the 'ordinary' knighthood, the Knight Bachelor, who was a member of no particular Order of Chivalry. It was extremely rare for a naval officer to receive a knighthood in this form.

The Order of the British Empire was instituted by King George V in 1917 to provide recognition for all subjects, regardless of rank or status. For members of the armed forces, there were five grades which were awarded to commissioned officers: Member (MBE), Officer (OBE), Commander (CBE), and KBE, and GBE as for the senior orders (NB, the difference between the title of the third grade of this Order, 'Commander', whereas for the other Orders the third grade is 'Companion'.) Ratings could be awarded the British Empire Medal (BEM). In 1997, the rules were changed to bring more equality. Ratings as well as officers may now be awarded the MBE, and the BEM has disappeared.

There are other, senior, honours, such as the Order of Merit (OM) and

Companion of Honour (CH), but naval officers are not often included among them. There have been eleven naval OMs in this century, all Admirals of the Fleet: Seymour, Fisher, Wilson, Jellicoe, Beatty, Madden, Chatfield, Pound, Cunningham of Hyndhope, Prince Philip, Duke of Edinburgh, and Mountbatten (plus, to be absolutely accurate, Professor Lord Blackett, who started his career as a naval officer).

At the beginning of the twentieth century there were only two awards for bravery or distinguished service. The first was, and remains, the Victoria Cross (VC), which takes precedence over all other honours, of whatever nature, and which is awarded to officers and men alike of the armed forces for bravery beyond the call of duty in the face of the enemy. The second was the Distinguished Service Order (DSO), which was awarded, to officers of the armed forces only, for meritorious service while on active service: this included bravery in the field, but was not exclusively for brave conduct.

During the First World War a number of other awards were instituted for bravery or distinguished conduct while on active service. In particular, there were six awards, two for each of the armed services (the Royal Air Force coming into existence on 1 April 1918), and each service had a Cross for an officer's award, and a Medal for an other rank's award. The Royal Navy's awards were, and remain, the Distinguished Service Cross (DSC) and Distinguished Service Medal (DSM). There will also be found naval officers who were in the Fleet Air Arm, who were awarded the Air Force equivalent, the Distinguished Flying Cross (DFC).

Other awards which may be encountered were the Air Force Cross (AFC), for meritorious service in the air, not in the face of the enemy, and the George Medal (GM, awarded to servicemen or civilians for bravery, not in the presence of the enemy). And to clarify matters slightly (it is hoped), the George Cross (GC) was the civilian equivalent of the VC, and takes precedence accordingly, but obviously will not be found among the awards to servicemen (though there is at least one instance of a naval Lieutenant being awarded the Albert Medal (later transferred to the George Cross) while on secondment to a scientific expedition).

This list is not exhaustive, but covers the majority of honours and awards which were received by naval officers in the twentieth century. Many naval officers also received awards from foreign nations, and their acceptance had to be approved by the sovereign. Such awards did not carry 'post-nominals' after a recipient's name, and usually they were only worn on an appropriate occasion in the country which awarded them, or in this country in the presence of the other country's representative.

Some, but not necessarily all, have been listed here. There were also 'mentions in dispatches', which recognized what were (in official eyes, at least) lesser degrees of bravery or meritorious service. Such an award carried no entitlement to letters after the recipient's name, but was recognized by a small bronze oak leaf worn on the appropriate medal ribbon (see below).

There were campaign medals, which merely indicated that the recipient had served in the appropriate theatre of war or in a particular campaign. The Oak Leaf badge, signifying a Mention in Despatches was worn on the ribbon of the campaign in which it was awarded. They are never listed with an individual's name, but some of the campaign medals awarded at the end of the nineteenth century are included, because their recipients themselves listed them in descriptions of their careers.

We have also included the award of Good Service Pensions (GSP). These were a form of financial bonus, awarded in two classes. A Captain's GSP was for £150 p.a., and was awarded to selected Captains as they approached the top of the Captain's List. Often the award was coincidental (or very nearly so) with the appointment as AdC (see below). The 'pension' was only paid while one was a Captain, so if one became a Flag Officer, one received it for barely a year. The other GSP was a Flag Officer's GSP, of £300 p.a., paid for life. There was a limit to the number of GSPs of both classes paid, so one had to wait until the most senior had retired or been promoted, in the case of the Captain's GSP, while for Flag Officer's, it was very literally 'dead men's shoes'. The amount paid remained at £150 and £300 throughout the century, until they were abolished with the coming of the Military Salary in the early 1970s. So, in the record, the entry GSP and a date may be taken as being a GSP of £150 (if he was a Captain at the time), payable from the date given until he was promoted to Rear-Admiral, or a GSP of £300 (if he was an Admiral at the time), payable from the date given until death.

Finally, we have included the appointments of officers as Aides-de-Camp to the monarch. When originally established (pre-1810), an Aide-de-Camp to the monarch carried the equivalent rank of Colonel in the Army. Later, senior officers of Colonel/Captain, RN's rank were appointed AdC to the monarch as a form of recognition; the appointment carried with it no practical duties, other than attendance on the monarch if one was in his or her orbit on a naval occasion. But, note, the AdC to, say, a General was his general factotum and was usually of (Army) Captain's rank. In the Navy, the equivalent was the Admiral's Flag Lieutenant (not surprisingly, of (Navy) Lieutenant's rank). Captains RN, approaching the top of the Captains' List, were selected and appointed AdC usually when they had less than two years to serve before becoming eligible for Flag rank. On being promoted to Rear-Admiral, they relinquished the appointment. The appointment as AdC was initially honorary, but prior to the Second World War an AdC could expect to be advanced to being a paid AdC. We have not noted this difference.

At the start of the century, there were ten AdCs to the monarch at any time. In 1951, there were still ten; by 1975 the number had increased to twelve; in 2000, there were eight. In strict terms, the appointment AdC carries no post-nominals, but it seems to have become the usage (possibly through ignorance) for officers to use AdC while holding the appointment, after their name and any other decorations they may hold. The badge of rank of the AdC when in ceremonial uniform is a set of aiguillettes, worn on the right shoulder (a Flag Lieutenant wears a set on the left shoulder).

There is also an appointment for a senior Admiral as First and Principal Naval ADC to the monarch. Until 1972 the appointment was given to a senior Admiral other than the First Sea Lord. Since 1972 the appointment has been vested in the office of First Sea Lord and Chief of Naval Staff. It does have certain ceremonial duties, and the post-nominals ADC are used while the officer holds the appointment.

Dates

The date given for an award is that of its being gazetted (announced in the *London Gazette*).

Since this is a biography of people's service in the Royal Navy, it will be found that the entry in the heading of 'On Leaving' (name and style, including post-nominals for decorations) does not always reflect their later style, e.g. an officer leaving the Active List as a Rear-Admiral, who is subsequently promoted on the Retired List, and who may have been correctly and generally known in retirement as Admiral Sir John Smith, will appear in these entries as Rear-Admiral John Smith. And decorations awarded after retirement will not appear in this particular entry, though, as a rule, a complete list, including honours granted after retirement, will appear in the 'Honours and Awards' section. These might include officers who became colonial Governors on retirement, earning, say, a KCMG. We have, however, included in the 'On Leaving' entry honours granted shortly after leaving, in respect of service in the final naval appointment. Examples include Admirals who usually retired having been awarded a KCB on their way through the Flag List, and who were promoted to GCB shortly after leaving their final appointment.

The nature of the honour or award

In gazetting an award, there would be a brief citation of what the award was for. In the case of VCs, GCs, GMs and often DSOs the citation might be quite extensive. But mostly it was fairly general. We may cite as an example the award of a DSC to Lieutenant-Commander Phillip Somerville, gazetted on 23 December 1939 among half a dozen others, 'for successful actions against enemy submarines'. In fact, his ship, the destroyer *Kingston*, had been one of three which had together hunted and sunk U-235, and the DSC was his reward, one might say, for having been responsible for training and leading a successful fighting machine which had destroyed one of the King's enemies, rather than for a specific act of bravery.

Some honours were similarly gained. The basic Companionship of the Order of the Bath was sometimes given to the successful Captain of an individual ship, though as a general rule, the DSO was a more likely award. Since there is an order of precedence in honours and awards (as shown by the order in which the post-nominal letters appear after a name), so, in general terms, the greater the service, the higher the honour.

Many honours were given for little more than long service. This is not to denigrate them, but it is a fact that, for example, it was 'standard' by the 1960s for every Rear-Admiral to receive the CB shortly after he had completed his first Flag appointment, as a reflection of the long and meritorious service which had led to his selection for Flag rank.

Similarly, it would seem, sometimes an OBE, say, would be awarded to an officer who had not been selected for promotion as a 'consolation prize'. He had worked long and meritoriously, hoping to be selected for further promotion, but had not been selected. This was not through any particular shortcoming on his part, but because there were always more candidates for higher rank than there were positions, and someone had to come second.

It could fairly be said that, in peacetime anyway, if an award were gazetted in either of the half-yearly Honours' lists (New Year's Honours' List; Queen's (King's) Birthday's Honours' List), then the award was one for long and meritorious service. If it were made at some other time, then it was for some more particular service.

During the latter half of the twentieth century, there was a distinct 'pecking order' for the award of such 'long service Honours'. Lieutenant-Commanders and below received an MBE; Commanders, an OBE; Captains, a CBE. As mentioned above, Flag Officers were awarded a more senior honour, the CB, while one was unlikely to receive a knighthood until one reached Vice-Admiral's rank. And at that level there is no doubt that there were (in some people's eyes, anyway) 'first-class knighthoods' (KCB) and 'second-class knighthoods' (KBE). One First Sea Lord in the latter half of the century recorded in his memoirs that he was unwilling to recommend the award of the KCB to a non-seaman officer, though content that he should receive the KBE. And there have been examples of officers receiving honours in more than one order, for example, Admiral Sir James Somerville, who had received a 'routine' KCB as CinC East Indies in 1939, was awarded the KBE for his very considerable services in command of Force H in the Mediterranean in 1940–41. (This resulted in the well-known signal from Admiral Cunningham 'Fancy, twice a Knight, and at your age. Congratulations.') Similarly, the award of the KBE, rather than the KCB, to a Flag Officer commanding a foreign station was a pretty good indication that he would not receive further promotion (though this is not infallible – Admiral Sir William Andrewes only received the KBE, for his services as CinC West Indies, but went on to be an Admiral, though not appointed to a mainstream post (Sea Lord, or one of the Home Commands: Nore, Portsmouth, Plymouth).

There are, as ever, exceptions to the above generalities, but it may be said that if, for example, one encounters a Rear-Admiral with the OBE he probably received it when he was a Commander.

The 1990s saw many changes in the Honours and Awards system. The differentiation between officer and rating for bravery awards (DSC and DSM) was removed. And the award of honours for little more than long and meritorious service was discontinued.

Finally, it must be said that there have been officers who have refused an honour which has been offered, for personal reasons. The more honour to them.

9 General Remarks

First section 'Remarks': these comments are merely notes to help with the interpretation of the previous data, and are drawn from many sources, including service records, obituaries, (auto)biographies, etc. Their fullness (or otherwise) is dependent entirely on the sources the compiler has had access to, and his subjective assessment of what may be considered interesting.

10 Family

Since this is a 'Naval Biography', no real attempt has been made to record family matters in any detail, though one or two correspondents have provided more detailed comments. One particular aspect which has been covered is to record parentage and progeny, which will reveal to what extent the Navy has been (and to some extent remains) a family business. The obituarist of *The Daily Telegraph* (then Captain Peter Hore, RN) wrote of Sir Desmond Dreyer, 'His father, Admiral Sir Frederic Dreyer, was Jellicoe's flag captain in the battleship *Iron Duke* during the First World War and Inspector of Merchant Navy Gunnery in the Second. Dreyer maintained that the royalties from his father's gunnery inventions paid for his education at Dartmouth … Young Desmond specialized in the family business of gunnery, becoming squadron gunnery officer …' There have been many such dynasties (the third Dreyer became a communications officer, retiring as a Captain).

It may be of interest to social historians to see how many of our subjects changed their names to add a hyphenated section to their surnames. Some (Atkinson to Atkinson-Willes, for example) were to satisfy some testamentary requirement. But it has to be said (some will say, unkindly) that many seem to have been for purely social reasons (Smith to Bowden-Smith, Calthorpe to Gough-Calthorpe, Hall to King-Hall, and several others, and Jones to Tudor: there were many more).

Most of the details given in the family section are derived from *Who's Who*, or *Who Was Who*. We have only given details of parentage where the father's profession is clear.

By and large, naval officers were drawn from the middle class. (It may be suggested that no one can define the middle class, but everyone knows a middle-class person when they see one!) They were the sons of officers in the Services, the sons of professional men, quite often sons of churchmen. Until 1914, and to a lesser extent up until 1939, it was desirable for a naval officer, if he wanted to make a success of his profession (and certainly if he wanted to support a family), to have a private income – not a large one, but, say, about 50 per cent of his naval pay (and this latter was certainly not generous). One found the younger sons of the landed gentry and the lesser nobility, but there were relatively few titled officers in the Navy, other than those who were rewarded with a peerage for their naval or other services – the latter totalling sixteen.

11 Sources

Personal record (service record)

The definitive source for details for a naval officer's career must be his personal record, which was maintained by Admiralty clerks in the Second Sea Lord's department. After he left the Active List, his record remained in the Admiralty files, until it was placed in the National Archives (formerly the Public Record Office). At the time of writing (2013), records are only accessible to the public for those officers who joined the Navy up to and including 1917. This covers fifty of the sixty-three Admirals of the Fleet, and 200 of the 273 Admirals. This compiler has been privileged to have access to the service records of most of the other admirals who joined after 1917 but who are now deceased. For those still living, it has been possible to approach most of them to ask them to check their records and confirm the account of their career given by the *Navy List*.

The format of the service record changed from time to time during the period. Thus the wording used for an appointment as, say, Second Sea Lord may be different comparing 1890 and 1990. Nor was it always as complete as it should have been. In general it gives full details of the dates of an officer's appointment to his succession of ships and shore appointments/courses, and his rank and seniority, but it does not always say where his ship was serving, nor when his appointment ended: for that the easiest source is the *Navy List*, although a more reliable source, available up to 1913, was the *List of HM Ships in Commission*. And care must be taken in reconciling the dates given in the service record and the *Navy List* (they frequently differ – as indeed they do in the different sections of his service record). The notation ADM/xxx/yy in the Sources section of these records indicate that the officer's service record in The National Archives as Kew has been used as the primary source. 'Service Record – MoD source (not yet in National Archives)' means exactly what it says.

And it must be said that any idea that all the Admiralty clerks wrote in a beautiful copperplate hand should be banished at once. The ADM/196/14 series which covered an officer's career from entry to retirement for those who joined prior to 1870 is an honourable exception, but the ADM/196/36 series which overlaps the ADM/196/14 series, and gives greater detail of appointments, and reports on an officer's abilities is, in general, written in an execrable hand. In many cases it is only possible to decipher what has been written by knowing standard phraseology and knowing the nature of the ship or establishment and its tasks. And many of the records have become physically damaged, or are missing in part.

The *Navy List*

The next most reliable source is the *Navy List*, an official publication produced by the Admiralty (later the Ministry of Defence (Navy)). In the 1850s, which is effectively the earliest that any of our subjects joined, it was published quarterly; by the 1890s it was published monthly, and continued so until December 1940, when it became every two months. At the end of 1944, it reverted to quarterly publication, remaining so until January 1957, when it became twice a year, with condensed issues in the intervening quarters. Finally, from 1976 it became an annual publication. Since 2010 it has no longer been published in hard copy.

The amount of information available has fluctuated over the years. There has always been an alphabetical list of every officer in the Service, giving his name, initials, any decorations, current rank and seniority in that rank, branch or specialization and where serving. There has always been a seniority list, which gave, in rank order from the top down, in order of seniority in each rank, his or her full name, Christian names, decorations and additional qualifications, together with his seniority, branch/specialization and specialization/sub-specialization. Until 1957 there was also a list of ships in and out of commission, with the name of every officer, down to Cadet, who was serving in each ship and the date on which he was appointed. From 1957 until 1980 the list of ships' officers was restricted to heads of departments. From 1981 onwards, for some five years, no officers were named with any ship, but by 1986, with one or two exceptions, the list of ship's officers contained at least the Captain's name. And until the Second World War, the ship's unit (e.g. 5th Cruiser Squadron), and station, and manning depot were included. After the Second World War that detail disappeared.

At various dates, much other information has been available from the *Navy List*. There have been comprehensive lists of the holders of various honours and awards; in the First World War, casualty lists were published (but not in the Second World War). There have been lists of officers holding interpreters' qualifications, and hydrographic surveying qualifications; the class of pass gained in the examinations for lieutenant, etc. Broadly speaking, the maximum amount of information was obtainable from the *Navy List* in the years 1900–1939. From 1957 onwards it has been, for the naval historian, downhill all the way, until today's *Navy List* is, frankly, scarcely worth the paper on which it is printed (or today, the website on which it appears).[4]

Other *Navy Lists*

From about 1873 a semi-official publication, known variously as the *Royal Navy List*, or *Lean's Navy List* (after the compiler, Lt-Col Francis Lean, RMLI), was produced regularly, at varying intervals, until the Second World War. It contained much the same information as the Admiralty-published *Navy List*s, though in a slightly different format, but also

4 For example, in 2008 no given names were included, merely initials, which does not help to determine the sex of an officer. Even in these days of equality, it may be safely asserted that this is a vital piece of information.

contained a great deal more. In particular, it contained details of an officer's date of entry, and seniority as a Naval Cadet and Midshipman,[5] and, for senior officers, the date of their retirement. It also included details (based solely on information supplied by the officer himself) of 'war and meritorious services, honours and rewards, etc.' Some of these may seem extremely trivial (and by their inclusion may be thought to reveal an officer's values), but they also reveal greater detail of minor campaigns and actions at sea which appear in very few other histories.

Dictionary of National Biography

Although giving a good general impression of an officer's career, few entries in the DNB give a complete picture – nor is that the DNB's purpose. And the DNB usually contains more detail on the subject's interaction with other personalities and situations than will be found here.

Who's Who and Who Was Who

This is invaluable for dates, though since it relies largely on the subjects providing them it is not always complete (many subjects merely give no more than their year of birth, for example), and it is good for family details and the year in which honours and awards were received.

The London Gazette

This is the primary source for details of honours and awards, giving the date of the award, and also a citation for why the award was given (though some citations are extremely general).

It may be assumed that all the above have been used as source material, and except for the Personal Record details, they are not cited separately in the list of sources in each individual record. Thus the latter includes only details of the service record and extraordinary sources. If the service record is not available, then the notation 'Navy Lists, etc.' is used.

Most of the published records listed above can be consulted through the public library service, and some (the DNB, Who's Who and the London Gazette) are available free online through a few county library services.

List of HM Ships in Commission

This is the Victorian and Edwardian equivalent of the later 'Pink List', which showed the disposition of HM Ships around the world. It was not a public document, but can be accessed through the library of the National Museum of the Royal Navy, at Portsmouth, and the Naval Historical Branch, also at Portsmouth.

5 Date of entry never figured in the *Navy List*, nor prior to 1870 did Midshipmen appear in the *Navy List*. Thus if access to an officer's official record is not available, *Lean's List* is invaluable for details of late nineteenth-century careers.

Jane's Fighting Ships, Conway's All the World's Fighting Ships, **Colledge's** *Ships of the Royal Navy*

All the above provide details, in varying degrees, of the ships which provide the – not background, but foreground – in which an officer's career is grounded.

The *Retired List,* **the** *Appendix to the Navy List*

Until the Second World War, the *Retired List* was incorporated in the *Navy List* at six-monthly intervals. From 1944 onwards, it has appeared separately. The *Appendix to the Navy List* was originally incorporated in the *Navy List,* and contained such details as pay and half-pay rates and regulations, rules for retirements, etc.

Published autobiographies and biographies

Until about 1960, it was quite common for senior officers to write their own autobiographies, or autobiographical reminiscences. The compiler of this volume has been making his own collection: their value varies! Similarly, the obituaries, particularly in *The Times* and the *Daily Telegraph,* are of great use in filling in gaps in careers.

The *Naval Review*

The *Naval Review* is the Navy's professional journal, available by subscription. Its material is largely concerned with the naval problems of the day, but it also publishes recollections and reminiscences of its subscribers. A number of these have been cited in our text, and can be accessed through www.naval-review.co.uk/archive.asp.

Private collections

This compiler has been fortunate enough to be given, by David Stevens of the Naval Historical Department in the Navy Department, Canberra, the collection of cuttings of naval appointments from *The Times* and the *Daily Telegraph* made by the late Commander Anthony Gould, RANR. Commander Gould (who, quite coincidentally, was at school with this compiler), collected these cuttings dating from 1952 through to 1988, which greatly help to amplify details of appointments in the latter part of the century, as the *Navy List* itself ceased to provide them.

Cross-references

We have not used the notation (qv) each time another officer's name is mentioned. It may be taken that the other officer's name appears as another entry in this volume.

Accuracy of the records

All the official publications contain petty inaccuracies and errors, due to changes of appointments, due to 'the exigencies of the Service', transcription errors, etc. The *DNB* is not without blemish, either, while *Who Was Who,* in relying on the subjects themselves for details, is not always 100 per cent accurate.

In consequence, the accuracy given here may not be 100 per cent, though we have tried to cross-check details. If any reader has noted errors, we apologize, and will be pleased to receive corrections via the publisher.

Twentieth-Century Admirals of the Fleet

Alphabetical list

Name	Seniority	Reference No.
ASHMORE, Sir Edward Beckwith, GCB, DSC	9 February 1977	A-01-00057
BATHURST, Sir David Benjamin, GCB	10 July 1995	B-01-00063
BEATTY, Earl, GCB, OM, GCVO, DSO, DCL	3 April 1919	B-01-00019
BEGG, Sir Varyl Cargill, GCB, DSO, DSC	12 August 1968	B-01-00053
BOYLE, Sir William, KCB	21 January 1938	B-01-00036
(Later CORK & ORRERY, The Earl of, GCB, GCVO)		
BROCK, Sir Osmond de Beauvoir, GCB, KCMG, KCVO, DCL	31 July 1929	B-01-00028
BURNEY, Sir Cecil, GCMG, KCB	24 November 1920	B-01-00022
CALLAGHAN, Sir George Astley, GCB, GCVO	2 April 1917	C-01-00017
CHATFIELD, Sir Alfred Ernle Montacute, GCB, KCMG, CVO, DCL	8 May 1935	C-01-00032
(Subsequently CHATFIELD, Lord, PC, GCB, OM, KCMG, CVO, DCL)		
CLANWILLIAM, Rt Hon. Richard James, Earl of, GCB, KCMG	20 February 1895	C-01-00002
CREASY, Sir George Elvey, GCB, CBE, DSO, MVO	22 April 1955	C-01-00049
CUNNINGHAM, Sir Andrew Brown, Bt, GCB, DSO**	21 January 1943	C-01-00039
(Subsequently CUNNINGHAM of Hyndhope, Viscount, KT, GCB, OM, DSO**)		
CUNNINGHAM, Sir John Henry Dacres, GCB, MVO	21 January 1948	C-01-00042
De ROBECK, Sir John Michael, Bt, GCB, GCMG, GCVO	24 November 1925	D-01-00026
EDINBURGH, His Royal Highness the Duke of (see MOUNTBATTEN, Philip)		

ERSKINE, Sir James Elphinstone, KCB	3 October 1902	E-01-00006
FANSHAWE, Sir Arthur Dalrymple, GCVO, KCB	30 April 1910	F-01-00014
FIELD, Sir Frederick Laurence, GCB, KCMG	21 January 1933	F-01-00030
FIELDHOUSE, Sir John David Elliott, GCB, GBE	2 August 1985	F-01-00060
(Subsequently FIELDHOUSE of Gosport, Lord, GCB, GBE)		
FISHER, Sir John Arbuthnot, GCB, OM	4 December 1905	F-01-00010
(Subsequently FISHER of Kilverstone, Lord, GCB, OM, GCVO, LLD)		
FORBES, Sir Charles Morton, GCB, DSO	8 May 1940	F-01-00038
FRASER of North Cape, Lord, GCB, KBE	22 October 1948	F-01-00043
(GOUGH-)CALTHORPE, Hon. Sir Somerset Arthur, GCB, GCMG, CVO	8 May 1925	G-01-00025
HILL-NORTON, Sir Peter John, GCB	13 March 1971	H-01-00055
(Subsequently HILL-NORTON, Lord, GCB)		
HOTHAM, Sir Charles Frederick, GCB, GCVO	3 August 1903	H-01-00007
JACKSON, Sir Henry Bradwardine, GCB, KCVO, FRS, DSc, LLD	31 July 1919	J-01-00020
JELLICOE of Scapa, Viscount, GCB, OM, GCVO	3 April 1919	J-01-00018
(Subsequently JELLICOE of Scapa, Earl, GCB, OM, GCVO)		
JOHN, Sir Caspar, GCB	23 May 1962	J-01-00052
KELLY, Sir John Donald, KCB, CMG, MVO	12 July 1936	K-01-00034
KEPPEL, Hon. Sir Henry, GCB, DCL	5 August 1877	K-01-00001
KERR, Rt Hon. Lord Walter Talbot, GCB	16 June 1904	K-01-00008
KEYES, Sir Roger John Brownlow, Bt, GCB, KCVO, CMG, DSO, LLD, DCL	8 May 1930	K-01-00029
(Subsquently KEYES, Lord, GCB, KCVO, CMG, DSO, LLD, DCL)		
LAMBE, Sir Charles Edward, GCB, CVO	10 May 1960	L-01-00051
LAMBTON (later MEUX), Hon. Sir Hedworth, GCB, KCVO, MP	5 March 1915	L-01-00016
LEACH, Sir Henry Conyers, GCB	1 December 1982	L-01-00059
LE FANU, Sir Michael, GCB, DSC	30 July 1970	L-01-00054
LEWIN, Sir Terence Thornton, GCB, MVO, DSC	6 July 1979	L-01-00058
(Subsequently LEWIN of Greenwich, Lord, KG, GCB, MVO, DSC)		
LYONS, Sir Algernon McLennan, GCB	23 August 1897	L-01-00003
MADDEN, Sir Charles Edward, Bt, GCB, GCVO, KCMG, LLD	31 July 1924	M-01-00024
MAY, Sir William Henry, GCB, GCVO	20 March 1913	M-01-00015
McGRIGOR, Sir Rhoderick Robert, GCB, DSO, LLD	1 May 1953	M-01-00048
MEUX (see LAMBTON)		
MOUNTBATTEN of Burma, Earl, KG, PC, GCB, GCSI, GCIE, GCVO, DSO, LLD	22 October 1956	M-01-00050
MOUNTBATTEN, Philip, Duke of Edinburgh, KG, KT	15 January 1953	M-01-00047
NOEL, Sir Gerard Henry Uctred, KCB, KCMG	2 December 1908	N-01-00012
OLIVER, Sir Henry Francis, GCB, KCMG, MVO, LLD	21 January 1928	O-01-00027
OSWALD, Sir John Julian Robertson, GCB	2 March 1992	O-01-00062
POLLOCK, Sir Michael Patrick, GCB, MVO, DSC	1 March 1974	P-01-00056

POUND, Sir Alfred Dudley Pickman Rogers, GCB, GCVO	31 July 1939	P-01-00037
POWER, Sir Arthur John, GCB, GBE, CVO	22 April 1952	P-01-00045
RICHARDS, Sir Frederick William, GCB	29 November 1898	R-01-00004
SALMON, Sir Nowell, VC, GCB.	13 January 1899	S-01-00005
SEYMOUR, Sir Edward Hobart, GCB, OM, LLD	20 February 1905	S-01-00009
SOMERVILLE, Sir James Fownes, GCB, GBE, DSO	8 May 1945	S-01-00041
STAVELEY, Sir William Doveton Minet, GCB	25 May 1989	S-01-00061
STURDEE, Sir Frederick Charles Doveton, Bt, GCB, KCMG, CVO, LLD	5 July 1921	S-01-00023
TOVEY, Sir John Cronyn, GCB, KBE, DSO	22 October 1943	T-01-00040
(Subsequently TOVEY of Langton Matravers, Lord, GCB, KBE, DSO)		
TYRWHITT, Sir Reginald Yorke, Bt, GCB, DSO, DCL	21 July 1934	T-01-00031
VIAN, Sir Philip Louis, GCB, KBE, DSO, LLD	1 June 1952	V-01-00046
[WALES, His Royal Highness Albert Edward, Prince of, KG, KT, KP, GCB, GCSI, GCMG, GCIE, GCVO]	18 July 1887	HW-01-1
WESTER WEMYSS, Lord, GCB, CMG, MVO, DCL	1 November 1919	W-01-00021
WILLIS, Sir Algernon Usborne, GCB, KBE, DSO	20 March 1949	W-01-00044
WILSON, Sir Arthur Knyvet, VC, GCB, GCVO	1 March 1907	W-01-00011
WINDSOR, His Majesty King GEORGE V	7 May 1910	W-01-00013
WINDSOR, His Royal Highness Albert Edward Christian George Andrew Patrick David, Duke of, KG, KT, KP, GCSI, GCMG, GCIE, GCVO, GBE, MC	21 January 1936	W-01-00033
(Formerly His Majesty King Edward VIII)		
WINDSOR, His Majesty King GEORGE VI	11 December 1936	W-01-00035

Twentieth-Century Admirals

Alphabetical list

Name	Seniority	Reference No.
ABBOTT, Sir Peter Charles, GBE, KCB	3 October 1995	A-02-00272
ACLAND, Sir William Alison Dyke, Bt, CVO	22 March 1908	A-02-00039
ADAIR, Charles Henry	10 May 1913	A-03-00064
ADEANE, Edward Stanley, CMG	19 March 1898	A-02-00003
ALDRICH, Pelham, CVO	1 March 1907	A-02-00035
ALEXANDER(-SINCLAIR), Sir Edwyn Sinclair, KCB, MVO	4 October 1926	A-02-00116
ANDERSON, Sir Donald Murray, KCB, CMG, MVO	20 April 1931	A-02-00130
ANDREWES, Sir William Gerrard, KBE, CB, DSO	24 November 1954	A-02-00207
ATKINSON(-WILLES), Sir George Lambart, KCB	15 November 1908	A-02-00045
BACKHOUSE, Sir Roger, GCB, GCVO, CMG	11 February 1934	B-02-00140
BAILEY, Sir Sidney Robert, KBE, CB, CBE, DSO	31 July 1939	B-03-00159
BARLOW, Charles James, DSO	10 February 1911	B-02-00051
BATTENBERG, His Serene Highness Prince Louis Alexander of, GCB, GCVO, KCMG	13 July 1912	B-02-00059
(After 1917, MILFORD HAVEN, Marquess of, PC, GCB, GCVO, KCMG, LLD)		
BAYLY, Sir Lewis, KCB, CVO	25 October 1917	B-02-00087
BEAUMONT, Sir Lewis Anthony, KCB, KCMG	17 October 1906	B-02-00031
BEDFORD, Sir Frederick George Durham, GCB	3 October 1902	B-02-00014
BENTINCK, Sir Rudolf Walter, KCB, KCMG	5 April 1928	B-02-00121
BERESFORD, Rt Hon. Lord Charles William Delapoer, GCVO, KCB	11 November 1906	B-02-00032
BEST, Hon. Sir Matthew Robert, KCB, DSO, MVO	19 June 1936	B-02-00149
BETHELL, Hon. Sir Alexander Edward, KCB, KCMG	10 June 1916	B-02-00079

BICKFORD, Andrew Kennedy, CMG	22 March 1908	B-02-00038
BINGLEY, Sir Alexander Noel Campbell, GCB, OBE	17 August 1960	B-02-00220
BINNEY, Sir Thomas Hugh, KCB, DSO	6 April 1942	B-02-00168
BLACK, Sir John Jeremy, GBE, KCB, DSO	6 June 1989	B-02-00262
BOSANQUET, Sir Day Hort, KCB	4 December 1905	B-02-00030
(BOWDEN-)SMITH, Sir Nathaniel, KCB	26 October 1899	B-02-00007
BOYCE, Sir Michael Cecil, GCB, OBE	25 May 1995	B-02-00271
(Subsequently, Lord BOYCE of Pimlico, KG, GCB, OBE)		
BOYD, Sir Denis William, KCB, CBE, DSC	21 January 1948	B-02-00188
BRACKENBURY, John William, CB, CMG	8 June 1905	B-02-00028
BRADFORD, Sir Edward Eden, KCB, CVO	2 July 1917	B-02-00083
BRAND, Hon. Sir Hubert George, KCB, KCMG, KCVO	11 June 1928	B-02-00122
BRIDGE, Sir Cyprian Arthur George, KCB	30 August 1903	B-02-00019
(BRIDGEMAN-)SIMPSON, Sir Francis Charles Bridgeman, KCB	12 April 1911	B-02-00052
BRIGGS, Sir Charles John, KCB	10 January 1916	B-02-00076
BRIGSTOCKE, Sir John Richard, KCB	19 September 1997	B-02-00273
BRIND, Sir Eric James Patrick, KCB, CBE	20 March 1949	B-02-00191
BROCK, Sir Frederic Edward Errington, KCMG, CB	2 April 1917	B-02-00080
BROWN, Sir Brian Thomas, KCB, CBE	26 August 1989	B-02-00264
BROWNING, Sir Montague Edward, GCMG, KCB, MVO	1 November 1919	B-02-00098
BROWNRIGG, Sir Henry John Studholme, KBE, CB, DSO	15 May 1939	B-02-00157
BRUCE, Sir James Andrew Thomas, KCMG	8 February 1907	B-02-00034
BRYSON, Sir Lindsay Sutherland, KCB	1 August 1983	B-02-00254
BUCKLE, Claude Edward	6 August 1903	B-02-00017
BULLER, Sir Henry Tritton, KCVO, CB	1 April 1931	B-02-00129
BURMESTER, Rudolf Miles, CB, CMG	30 September 1933	B-02-00138
BURNETT, Sir Robert Lindsay, KCB, KBE, DSO, LLD	15 September 1946	B-02-00183
BURROUGH, Sir Harold Martin, GCB, KBE, DSO*	25 September 1945	B-02-00181
BUSH, Sir John Fitzroy Duyland, KCB, DSC**	20 August 1968	B-02-00234
BUSH, Sir Paul Warner, KCB, MVO	24 October 1915	B-02-00075
CARDEN, Sir Sackville Hamilton, KCMG	1 September 1917	C-02-00085
CASSELS, Sir Simon Alastair Cassilis, KCB, CBE	15 November 1984	C-02-00256
CASSIDI, Sir Arthur Desmond, GCB	27 September 1979	C-02-00251
CHARLTON, Sir Edward Francis Benedict, KCMG, CB	5 July 1921	C-02-00103
CHETWODE, Sir George, KCB, CBE	22 July 1936	C-02-00151
CLAYTON, Sir Richard Pilkington, GCB	24 March 1978	C-02-00248
CLINTON-BAKER, Sir Lewis, KCB, KCVO, CBE	8 November 1926	C-02-00118
COLVILLE, Hon. Sir Stanley Cecil James, KCB, CVO	11 September 1914	C-02-00072
COLVIN, Sir Ragnar Musgrave, KBE, CB	3 May 1939	C-02-00155
COUCHMAN, Sir Walter Thomas, KCB, CVO, DSO, OBE	30 April 1959	C-02-00217
COWAN, Sir Walter Henry, Bt, KCB, DSO, MVO	1 August 1927	C-02-00119
CRAIGIE, Robert William	2 July 1908	C-02-00043
CROSS, Charles Henry	16 May 1913	C-02-00066
(CULME-)SEYMOUR, Sir Michael, Bt, GCB	13 May 1893	C-02-00001
CURZON-HOWE, Hon. Sir Assheton Gore, GCVO, KCB, CMG	2 January 1909	C-02-00047

CUSTANCE, Sir Reginald Neville, KCB, KCMG, CVO	18 May 1908	C-02-00042
DALE, Alfred Taylor	30 May 1903	D-02-00016
DALRYMPLE-HAMILTON, Sir Frederick Hew George, KCB	4 January 1948	D-02-00187
DANIEL, Sir Charles Saumarez, KCB, CBE, DSO	1 May 1950	D-02-00194
DAVIS, Sir William Wellclose, GCB, DSO*	20 October 1956	D-02-00213
De CHAIR, Sir Dudley Rawson Stratford, KCB, MVO	25 November 1920	D-02-00100
DENISON, John	7 December 1913	D-02-00069
DENNY, Sir Michael Maynard GCB, CBE, DSO	22 April 1952	D-02-00201
DOMVILE, Sir Barry Edward KBE, CB, CMG	1 January 1936	D-02-00146
DOMVILE, Sir Compton Edward, KCB	5 January 1902	D-02-00013
DOUGLAS, Sir Archibald Lucius, KCB	2 March 1905	D-02-00027
DOUGLAS-PENNANT, Hon. Sir Cyril Eustace, KCB, CBE, DSO, DSC	26 January 1952	D-02-00198
DREYER, Sir Desmond Parry, KCB, CBE, DSC	5 June 1965	D-02-00228
DREYER, Sir Frederic Charles, KCB, CBE	31 December 1932	D-02-00135
DRUMMOND, Edward Charles	1 October 1903	D-02-00020
DRURY, Sir Charles Carter, GCVO, KCB, KCSI	11 April 1908	D-02-00040
DUFF, Sir Alexander Ludovic, KCB	1 July 1921	D-02-00102
DUFF, Sir Allan Arthur Morison, KCB	8 May 1930	D-02-00126
(DUNBAR-)NASMITH, Sir Martin Eric, VC, KCB	2 January 1936	D-02-00148
DURLACHER, Sir Laurence George, KCB, OBE, DSC	12 April 1961	D-02-00224
DURNFORD, Sir John, KCB, DSO	22 July 1910	D-02-00050
DURNFORD-SLATER, Sir Robin Leonard Francis, KCB	28 July 1959	D-02-00218
EASTON, Sir Ian, KCB, DSC	6 January 1976	E-02-00244
EATON, Sir Kenneth John, GBE, KCB	28 April 1993	E-02-00269
EBERLE, Sir James Henry Fuller, GCB	4 May 1979	E-02-00249
ECCLES, Sir John Arthur Symons, GCB, KCVO, CBE	1 December 1955	E-02-00210
EDELSTEN, Sir John Hereward, GCB, GCVO, CBE	3 February 1949	E-02-00190
EDWARD-COLLINS, Sir George Edward Basset, KCB, KCVO	21 January 1943	E-02-00173
EDWARDS, Sir Ralph Alan Bevan, KCB, CBE	22 April 1955	E-02-00209
EGERTON, Sir George Le Clerc, KCB	21 March 1913	E-02-00063
EMPSON, Sir Leslie Derek, GBE, KCB	1 August 1972	E-02-00240
ESSENHIGH, Sir Nigel Richard, KCB	11 September 1998	E-02-00274
EVANS, Sir Edward Ratcliffe Garth Russell, KCB, DSO	12 July 1936	E-02-00150
EVAN-THOMAS, Sir Hugh, GCB, KCMG, MVO, LLD	7 October 1920	E-02-00099
FANE, Sir Charles, KCB	24 January 1901	F-02-00009
FARQUHAR, Sir Arthur Murray, KCB, CVO	14 September 1914	F-02-00073
FARQUHAR, Richard Bowles, CB	5 October 1917	F-02-00086
FAWKES, Sir Wilmot Hawksworth, KCB, KCVO	12 October 1908	F-02-00044
FELLOWES, Sir John, KCB	20 November 1904	F-02-00025
FERGUSSON, Sir James Andrew, KCB, KCMG	25 October 1926	F-02-00117
FISHER, Sir Frederic William, KCVO	15 May 1913	F-02-00065
FISHER, Sir William Wordsworth, KCB, CVO	1 July 1932	F-02-00132
FITCH, Sir Richard George Alison KCB	3 January 1986	F-02-00258
FITZGERALD, Charles Cooper Penrose	20 February 1905	F-02-00026
FORD, Sir Wilbraham Tennyson Randle, KCB, KBE	31 January 1941	F-02-00165
FREMANTLE, The Hon. Sir Edmund Robert, GCB, CMG	10 October 1896	F-02-00002

FREMANTLE, Sir Sydney Robert, KCB, MVO	15 November 1922	F-02-00106
FREWEN, Sir John Byng, KCB	9 February 1966	F-02-00231
FULLER, Sir Cyril Thomas Moulden, KCB, CMG, DSO	15 May 1930	F-02- 00127
FULLERTON, Sir Eric Arthur, KCB, DSO, MA	31 August 1935	F-02-00144
GAMBLE, Sir Douglas Austin, KCVO	26 April 1917	G-02-00082
GAMBLE, Edward Harpur, CB	18 September 1911	G-02-00056
GAUNT, Sir Ernest Frederic Augustus, KCB, KBE, CMG	30 June 1924	G-02-00108
GIFFARD, George Augustus, CMG	19 July 1911	G-02-00054
GLADSTONE, Sir Gerald Vaughan, GBE, KCB	31 January 1958	G-02-00215
GOODENOUGH, Sir William Edmund, KCB, MVO	8 May 1925	G-02-00111
GOODRICH, Sir James Edward Clifford, KCVO	3 June 1913	G-02-00067
GRANT, Sir William Lowther, KCB	1 September 1918	G-02-00092
GRANTHAM, Sir Guy, GCB, CBE, DSO	22 October 1953	G-02-00206
GRIFFIN, Sir Anthony Templer Frederick Griffith, KCB	29 November 1971	G-02-00239
HAGGARD, Sir Vernon Stuart Harry, KCB, CMG	12 October 1932	H-02-00134
HALLIFAX, Sir David John, KCB, KBE	6 January 1986	H-02-00259
HAMILTON, Sir Frederick Tower KCB, CVO	9 June 1916	H-02-00077
HAMILTON, Sir John Graham, KBE, CB	11 August 1965	H-02-00230
HAMILTON, Sir Louis Henry Keppel, KCB, DSO*	16 May 1947	H-02-00184
HARCOURT, Sir Cecil Halliday Jepson, KCB, CBE	22 June 1949	H-02-00192
HARRIS, Sir Robert Hastings, KCB, KCMG	1 September 1904	H-02-00023
HEATH, Sir Herbert Leopold, KCB, MVO	30 October 1919	H-02-00097
HENDERSON, Sir Nigel Stuart, GBE, KCB	14 August 1963	H-02-00228
HENDERSON, Sir Reginald Friend Hannam, KCB	2 December 1908	H-02-00046
HENDERSON, Sir Reginald Guy Hannam, GCB	14 January 1939	H-02-00154
HERBERT, Sir Peter Geoffrey Marshall, KCB, OBE	10 June 1983	H-02-00253
HODGES, Sir Michael Henry, KCB, CMG, MVO	31 July 1929	H-02-00123
HOLLAND, Swinton Colthurst	1 June 1907	H-02-00036
HOLLAND-MARTIN, Sir Deric, KCB, DSO, DSC*	10 March 1961	H-02-00223
HOPE, Sir George Price Webley, KCB, KCMG	24 November 1925	H-02-00113
HOPKINS, Sir Frank Henry Edward, KCB, DSO, DSC	15 March 1966	H-02-00232
HORTON, Sir Max Kennedy, KCB, DSO**	9 January 1941	H-02-00164
HUNT, Sir Nicholas John Streynsham, GCB, LVO	6 August 1985	H-02-00257
INGLEFIELD, Sir Frederic Samuel, KCB	4 June 1913	I-02-00068
JACKSON, Sir Thomas Sturges, KCVO	5 July 1905	J-02-00029
JAMES, Sir William Milbourne, GCB	21 January 1938	J-02-00153
JEFFREYS, Edmund Frederick, CVO	18 May 1908	J-02-00041
JENKINGS, Albert Baldwin	1 January 1907	J-02-00033
JERRAM, Sir Thomas Martyn, KCB, CVO	10 April 1917	J-02-00081
KELLY, Sir William Archibald Howard, KCB, CMG, MVO	6 October 1931	K-02-00131
KENNEDY, Sir William Robert, GCB	16 June 1901	K-02-00011
KENNEDY-PURVIS, Sir Charles Edward, KCB	15 February 1942	K-02-00166
KERR, Sir John Beverley, GCB	26 November 1991	K-02-00267
KERR, Sir William Munro, KBE, CB	1 January 1936	K-02-00145
KINAHAN, Sir Harold Richard George, KBE, CB	1 December 1950	K-02-00196
(KING-)HALL, Sir George Fowler, KCB, CVO	19 May 1912	K-02 00058
(KING)-HALL, Sir Herbert Goodenough, KCB, CVO, DSO	25 August 1918	K-02-00091
LARKEN, Frank, CB, CMG	1 September 1933	L-02-00137

LAURENCE, Sir Noel Frank, KCB, DSO	1 August 1940	L-02-00163
LAW, Sir Horace Rochefort, GCB, OBE, DSC	17 September 1968	L-02-00235
LAYARD, Sir Michael Henry Gordon, KCB, CBE	1 September 1994	L-03-00269
LAYTON, Sir Geoffrey, KCB, DSO	15 September 1942	L-02-00170
LEATHAM, Sir Ralph, KCB	9 December 1943	L-02-00175
LEVESON, Sir Arthur Cavenagh, KCB	1 June 1922	L-02-00105
LEWIS, Sir Andrew Mackenzie, KCB	21 August 1971	L-02-00238
LIMPUS, Sir Arthur Henry, KCMG, CB	3 January 1918	L-02-00089
LITTLE, Sir Charles James Colebrooke, GCB, GBE	25 June 1937	L-02-00152
LIVESAY, Sir Michael Howard, KCB	3 May 1991	L-02-00266
LOWRY, Sir Robert Swinburne, KCB	13 December 1913	L-02-00071
LUCE, Sir John David, KCB, DSO*	22 August 1960	L-02-00221
LYGO, Sir Raymond Derek, KCB	9 February 1977	L-02-00246
LYON, Sir George Hamilton D'Oyly, KCB	15 June 1942	L-02-00169
MACLEOD, Angus, CVO	1 January 1910	M-02-00048
MADDEN, Sir Alexander Gordon Cumming, KCB, CBE	18 March 1953	M-02-00203
MADDEN, Sir Charles Edward, Bt, GCB	8 November 1961	M-02-00226
MANSERGH, Sir Maurice James, KCB, CBE	18 March 1953	M-02-00204
MARKHAM, Sir Albert Hastings, KCB	21 January 1903	M-02-00015
McKAIG, Sir John Rae, KCB, CBE	13 May 1974	M-02-00241
MEADE-FETHERSTONHAUGH, Hon. Sir Herbert, GCVO, CB, DSO	31 July 1934	M-02-00142
MEYRICK, Sir Sidney Julius, KCB	1 June 1940	M-02-00161
MILES, Sir Geoffrey John Audley, KCB, KCSI	4 January 1948	M-02-00186
MILFORD HAVEN – See BATTENBERG		
MILNE, Sir Archibald Berkeley, Bt, GCVO, KCB	19 September 1911	M-02-00057
MITCHELL, Francis Herbert, CB, DSO	21 January 1933	M-02-00136
MOLYNEUX, Sir Robert Henry More, KCB	13 July 1899	M-02-00006
MOORE, Sir Archibald Gordon Henry Wilson, KCB, CVO	17 January 1919	M-02-00095
MOORE, Sir Arthur William, KCB, KCVO, CMG	10 October 1907	M-02-00037
MOORE, Sir Henry Ruthven, GCB, CVO, DSO	15 April 1945	M-02-00179
MORANT, George Digby	13 March 1901	M-02-00008
MORTON, Sir Anthony Storrs, GBE, KCB	6 July 1979	M-02-00250
NEVILLE, Sir George, KCB, CVO	30 July 1912	N-02-00060
NICHOLSON, Sir Douglas Romilly Lothian, KCMG, KCVO	10 March 1925	N-02-00110
NICHOLSON, Sir William Coldingham Masters, KCB	7 July 1925	N-02-00112
NOBLE, Sir Percy Lockhart Hannam, KCB, CVO	3 May 1939	N-02-00156
NORTH, Sir Dudley Burton Napier, KCVO, CB, CSI, CMG	8 May 1940	N-02-00162
O'BRIEN, Sir William Donough, KCB, DSC	4 April 1970	O-02-00236
OLIVER, Sir Geoffrey Nigel, GBE, KCB, DSO**	15 May 1952	O-02-00202
ONSLOW, Sir Richard George, KCB, DSO***	31 January 1959	O-02-00216
OXLEY, Charles Lister	16 June 1904	O-02-00022
PACKER, Sir Herbert Annesley, KCB, CBE	15 March 1952	P-02-00199
PAGET, Sir Alfred Wyndham, KCB, KCMG	8 December 1913	P-02-00070
PAKENHAM, Sir William Christopher, KCB, KCMG, KCVO	6 April 1922	P-02-00104
PALLISER, Sir Arthur Francis Eric, KCB, DSC	16 May 1947	P-02-00185
PARHAM, Sir Frederick Robertson, GBE, KCB, DSO	29 February 1956	P-02-00211

PARKER, Henry Wise, CB, CMG	10 October 1933	P-02-00139
PARRY, Sir William Edward, KCB	1 May 1951	P-02-00197
PATEY, Sir George Edwin, KCMG, KCVO	1 January 1918	P-02-00088
PATTERSON, Sir Wilfrid Rupert, KCB, CVO, CBE	30 August 1949	P-02-00193
PEARSON, Sir Hugo Lewis, KCB	20 October 1904	P-02-00024
PEIRSE, Sir Richard Henry, KCB, KBE, MVO	11 March 1918	P-02-00090
PELHAM, Frederick	9 June 1916	P-02-00078
PEROWNE, Sir James Francis, KBE	9 May 2000	P-02-00275
PHILLIMORE, Sir Richard Fortescue, KCB, KCMG, MVO	01 August 1924	P-02-00109
PILLAR, Sir William Thomas, GBE, KCB	5 January 1982	P-02-00252
PIZEY, Sir Charles Thomas Mark, GBE, CB, DSO*	16 December 1954	P-02-00208
PLUNKETT(-ERNLE-ERLE-DRAX), The Hon. Sir Reginald Aylmer Ranfurly, KCB, DSO	2 January 1936	P-02-00147
POË, Sir Edward Samuel, KCB, KCVO	30 April 1910	P-02-00049
POORE, Sir Richard, Bt, KCB, CVO	17 July 1911	P-02-00053
PORTAL, Sir Reginald Henry, KCB, DSC	4 October 1950	P-02-00195
POWER, Sir Manley Laurence, KCB, CBE, DSO*	22 July 1960	P-02-00219
PRESTON, Sir Lionel George, KCB	28 February 1934	P-02-00141
PRIDHAM-WIPPELL, Sir Henry Daniel, KCB, DSO	30 June 1944	P-02-00178
RAIKES, Sir Robert Henry Taunton, KCB, CVO, DSO*	29 October 1942	R-02-00172
RAMSAY, The Hon. Sir Alexander Robert Maule, GCVO, KCB, DSO	15 December 1939	R-02-00160
RAMSAY, Sir Bertram Home, KCB, KBE, MVO	27 April 1944	R-O2-00177
RAMSEY, Sir Charles Gordon, KCB	6 April 1942	R-02-00167
RAWSON, Sir Harry Holdsworth, KCB	12 August 1903	R-02-00018
REFFELL, Sir Derek, KCB	28 September 1988	R-02-00261
REID, Sir Peter John Lorne GCB, CVO	7 January 1958	R-02-00214
RICE, Ernest	15 March 1904	R-02-00021
RICHMOND, Sir Herbert William, KCB	6 October 1929	R-02-00124
ROBINSON, Charles Grey, CVO	27 August 1911	R-02-00055
ROYLE, Sir Guy Charles Cecil, KCB, CMG	29 October 1942	R-02-00171
RUSSELL, Hon. Sir Guy Herbrand Edward, GBE, KCB, DSO	10 April 1952	R-02-00200
SCOTT, Rt Hon. Lord Charles Thomas Montagu Douglas, KCB	30 June 1899	S-02-00005
SCOTT, Sir Percy Moreton, KCVO, CB, LLD	20 March 1913	S-02-00062
SCOTT-MONCRIEFF, Sir Alan Kenneth, KCB, CBE, DSO*	30 June 1956	S-02-00212
SIMONS, Ernest Alfred	24 October 1914	S-02-00074
SINGER, Sir Morgan, KCVO, CB	03 March 1924	S-02-00107
SLADE, Sir Edmond John Warre, KCIE, KCVO	19 August 1917	S-02-00084
SLATER, Sir John Cunningham Kirkwood, GCB, LVO	20 January 1991	S-02-00265
SLAYTER, Sir William Rudolph, KCB, DSO, DSC	15 September 1953	S-02-00205
ST. JOHN, Henry Craven	15 June 1901	S-02-00010
STANFORD, Sir Peter Maxwell, KCB, MVO	14 February 1985	S-02-00255
STANLEY, Hon. Sir Victor Albert KCB, MVO	2 March 1926	S-02-00115
STEPHENSON, Sir Henry Frederick, KCB	7 December, 1901	S-02-00012
SYFRET, Sir Edward Neville, GCB, KBE	1 February 1946	S-02-00182
TAIT, Sir Allan Gordon, KCB, DSC	14 March 1978	T-02-00247
TENNANT, Sir William George, KCB, CBE, MVO	22 October 1948	T-02-00189

THESIGER, Sir Bertram Sackville, KBE, CB, CMG	23 September 1932	T-02-00133
THOMAS, Sir William Richard Scott, KCB, OBE	1 August 1989	T-02-00263
THURSBY, Sir Cecil Fiennes KCB, KCMG	9 April 1919	T-02-00096
TOTHILL, Sir Hugh Henry Derby, KCMG, KCVO, CB	1 March 1926	T-02-00114
TOTTENHAM, Sir Francis Loftus, KCB, CBE	28 June 1939	T-02-00158
TRACEY, Sir Michael Edward, KCB	29 November 1898	T-02-00004
TREACHER, Sir John Devereux, KCB	15 December 1975	T-02-00243
TROUBRIDGE, Sir Ernest Charles Thomas, KCMG, CB, MVO	9 January 1919	T-02-00094
TUDOR, Sir Frederick Charles Tudor, KCB, KCMG	16 May 1921	T-02-00101
TUPPER, Sir Reginald Godfrey Otway, KCB, CVO	1 January 1919	T-02-00093
TURNER, Sir Arthur Francis, KCB, DSC	21 April 1970	T-02-00237
TWEEDIE, Sir Hugh Justin, KCB	8 May 1935	T-02-00143
TWISS, Sir Frank Roddam, KCB, DSC	26 December 1967	T-02-00233
TYRWHITT, St John Reginald Joseph, KCB, DSO, DSC*	9 September 1961	T-02-00225
WAISTELL, Sir Arthur Kipling, KCB	23 May 1930	W-02-00128
WAKE-WALKER, Sir William Frederic, KCB, CBE	8 May 1945	W-02-00180
WATSON, Sir Hugh Dudley Richards, KCB, CVO, CBE	9 October 1929	W-02-00125
WEBB, Sir Richard KCMG, CB	21 January 1928	W-02-00120
WELLS, Sir Lionel Victor, KCB, DSO	22 October 1943	W-02-00174
WEST, Sir Alan William John, KCB, DSC	3 November 2000	W-02-00276
WHITE, Sir Hugo Moresby, GCB, OBE	15 December 1992	W-02-00268
WHITE, Sir Peter, GBE	28 June 1976	W-02-00245
WHITWORTH, Sir William Jock, KCB, DSO	31 December 1943	W-02-00176
WILLIAMS, Sir David, GCB	8 September 1974	W-02-00242
WINSLOE, Sir Alfred Leigh, KCB, CVO, CMG	30 September 1912	W-02-00061
WOODS, Sir Wilfrid John Wentworth, KCB, DSO*	2 December 1960	W-02-00222
WOODWARD, Sir John Forster, GBE, KCB	21 July 1987	W-02-00260
WRIGHT, Sir Royston Hollis, GBE, KCB, DSC*	26 January 1962	W-02-00227

Twentieth-Century Honorary Admirals of the Fleet and Admirals

Alphabetical list

Name	Seniority	Reference No.
De BORBON y BATTENBERG, HRH Don Juan, Count of Barcelona	13 July 1987	HS-02-10
DENMARK, His Majesty King Christian X of, KG, GCB	27 November 1920	HD-02-5
DENMARK, His Majesty King Frederick IX of, KG, GCB, GCVO	17 September 1948	HD-02-6
HELLENES, His Majesty King George I of the, KG, GCVO	31 October 1901	HH-02-1
HELLENES, His Majesty King Paul of, GCVO	16 February 1953	HH-02-8
NORWAY, His Majesty King Haakon VII of, KG, GCB, GCVO	25 November 1905	HN-02-3
NORWAY, His Majesty King Olaf V of, KG, KT, GCB, GCVO	12 April 1988	HN-01-5
PORTUGAL AND THE ALGARVES, His Majesty King Charles I of, KG	28 September 1903	HP-02-3
PRUSSIA, His Royal Highness Prince Albert William Henry of, KG, GCB	27 January 1910	HP-01-4
PRUSSIA, His Imperial Majesty William II, German Emperor and King of, KG, GCVO	02 August 1889	HP-01-2
RUSSIAS, His Imperial Majesty Nicholas II, Emperor of all the, KG	1 June 1908	HR-01-3
SWEDEN, His Majesty King Gustavus V of, of the Goths and of the Vends, KG, GCB	3 November 1908	HS-02-4
SWEDEN, His Majesty King Gustavus VI Adolf of, of the Goths and the Vends, KG, GCB, GCVO	1 May 1951	HS-02-7
SWEDEN, His Majesty King Carl XVI Gustaf of, KG	25 June 1975	HS-02-9
WALES, His Royal Highness Albert Edward, Prince of, KG, KT, KP, GCB, GCSI, GCMG, GCIE, GCVO	18 July 1887	HW-01-1

Abbreviations and acronyms

We have tried to keep the use of initials, acronyms etc., to a minimum, but those which are used are as they appear in the *Navy List* of the relevant date. For many appointments in the latter half of the century, NATO (sorry, North Atlantic Treaty Organisation) condensed titles are used.

1SL	First Sea Lord
2SL	Second Sea Lord
3SL	Third Sea Lord – more usually known as the Controller
4SL	Fourth Sea Lord
5SL	Fifth Sea Lord
ABCD	Atomic, Bacteriological and Chemical Defence
ABC and DC	Atomic, Bacteriological and Chemical and Damage Control
ACDS	Assistant Chief of Defence Staff
ACNS	Assistant Chief of Naval Staff
ACR	Admiral Commanding Reserves
ADC	(AdC) Aide de Camp to the current Monarch. (ADC is used for officers of Flag rank; AdC for Captains)
ADNI	Assistant Director, Naval Intelligence
AD&DC	Atomic Defence and Damage Control
AEW	Airborne Early Warning
AF	Admiral of the Fleet
AFO	Admiralty Fleet Order
AS	Admiral Superintendent (of a dockyard)
A/S	Anti-submarine
asc	Passed the Army Staff Course at Camberley (later psc(m))
ASCBS	Admiral Superintending Contract-Built Ships

ASW	Anti-submarine Warfare
AWI	America and West Indies (station) (this included South America)
AWO(A)	Advanced Warfare Officer (Above Water Warfare) (the equivalent of the old (G) officer)
AW	Amphibious Warfare
BPF	British Pacific Fleet (1944–46)
BR	Book of Reference
BS	Battle Squadron
BS1	The Flag Officer commanding the First Battle Squadron
(1BS	The First Battle Squadron)
BWK (Cert)	Bridge Watchkeeping Certificate: the Seaman officer's basic proof of competence
(C)	Communications specialist (formerly Signals (S))
CB (1)	Companion of the Order of the Bath
CB (2)	CB also was an everyday term for Confidential Book
CBNS	Commander British Naval Staff
CDS	Chief of the Defence Staff
CFS	Chief of Fleet Support (previously usually known as 4SL)
CinC	Commander-in-Chief
CINCAFMED	(NATO) Commander-in-Chief Allied Forces Mediterranean
CINCEASTLANT	(NATO) Commander-in-Chief Eastern Atlantic
CINCCHAN	(NATO) Commander-in-Chief Channel
CMS	Coastal Minesweeper
CNJA	Chief Naval Judge Advocate: a naval officer, head of the Navy's Law branch
COMASWSTRIKFOR	(NATO) Commander of the ASW Striking Force
COMEDSOUEAST	(NATO) Commander South East Area, Mediterranean
COMNORECHAN	(NATO) Commander Nore Area Channel Command. (In national terms, when CinC Nore was abolished, FOSNI took over the responsibilities.)
COMNORLANT	(NATO) Commander Northern Area, Atlantic Command
COMSTANAVFORLANT	(NATO) Commander Standing Naval Force Atlantic
COMSUBEASTLANT	(NATO) Commander of Submarines in the Eastern Atlantic area
COMUKTG	(NATO) Commander of the UK Task Group
COQC	Commanding Officers' Qualifying Course (for submarines) (the 'perisher')
CoS	Chief of Staff
CPE	Chief Polaris Executive
CS	Cruiser Squadron (see also LCS)
CSCBS	Commodore Superintending Contract-Built Ships
CSO	Chief Staff Officer
CVA	NATO designation of a Strike Aircraft Carrier
CVO	Companion of the Royal Victorian Order
(D)	Direction (or Fighter Direction) specialist

DCNS	Deputy Chief of Naval Staff
DF	Destroyer Flotilla
D/F	Direction Finding – a means of navigation using radio
(D)DNOT	Deputy Director Naval Operations and Trade
DGO	Destroyer Gunnery Officer
DGS	Director General (Ships)
DIS	Director, Intelligence Services
DLG	A Large Destroyer armed with Guided missiles
DNB	*Dictionary of National Biography*
DNC	Director of Naval Construction
DNCXF	Deputy Naval Commander, Expeditionary Force (Invasion of Sicily, 1943)
DNI	Director(ate) of Naval Intelligence (an Admiralty/MoD(N) department)
DNLD	Director, Naval Electrical Department (an Admiralty/MoD(N) department)
DNMT(S)	Director(ate) of Naval Manning and Training (Supply & Secretariat) (an Admiralty/MoD(N) department)
DNO	Director of Naval Ordnance (an Admiralty department)
DNOT	Director(ate) of Naval Operations and Trade (an Admiralty/MoD(N) department)
DNDO	Destroyer ND Officer. Generic term for non-long course officer as Navigating Officer of destroyer or frigate.
DNOA(S)	Director(ate) of Naval Officers' Appointments (Supply & Secretariat) (an Admiralty/MoD(N) department)
DNOA(X)	Director(ate) of Naval Officers' Appointments (Executive)
DOA(X)	The previous name of DNOA(X): the change was made with the formation of the MoD in April 1964.
DOD(F)	Director of Operations Division (Foreign) (an Admiralty department)
DOD(H)	Director of Operations Division (Home) (an Admiralty department)
DSC	Holder of the Distinguished Service Cross
DSD	Director of Signal Division (an Admiralty department)
DSO	Holder of the Distinguished Service Order
DTWP	Director(ate) of Tactical and Weapons Policy (an Admiralty department)
DNSY	Director(ate) of Naval Security (an Admiralty/MoD(N) department)
FAA	Fleet Air Arm
FC	Fighter Controller (the present equivalent of the old (D) officer)
FDO	Fighter Direction Officer (the forerunner of the (D) officer)
FGO	Fleet Gunnery Officer
FO	Flag Officer
FOAIB	Flag Officer Admiralty Interview Board

FO2FEF	Flag Officer, Second-in-Command, Far East Fleet
FO2FES	Flag Officer, Second-in-Command, Far East Station
FO2iC	Flag Officer Second-in-Command
FOF (1, 2 or 3)	Flag Officer 1st, 2nd or 3rd Flotilla (the three seagoing admirals of the 1970s and 80s)
FOFT & FOGT	Flag Officer Flying Training: Flag Officer Ground Training
FOFWF	Flag Officer, Flotillas, Western Fleet (the immediate predecessor of FOF 1, 2 or 3)
FOO (or FO(O))	Fleet Operations Officer
FORY	Flag Officer Royal Yachts
FOSNI	Flag Officer Scotland and Northern Ireland
FOST	Flag Officer Sea Training
FRAeS	Fellow of the Royal Aeronautical Society
FRGS	Fellow of the Royal Geographic Society
(G)	Gunnery specialist
(g)	An officer who has done a short gunnery course, to take charge of the armament in a small ship
GCB	Knight Grand Cross of the Order of the Bath
GOC	General Officer Commanding (an Army abbreviation)
GSP	Good Service Pension
hcsc	Passed the Higher Command and Staff Course
(H)	Hydrographic Surveying specialist: succeeded (1992) by –
(HM)	Hydrographic, Meteorological and Oceanographic specialist
HEO	Higher Executive Officer (a Civil Service rank)
HMMSC(E)	Her Majesty's Minesweeper Support Craft (Engineering)
IDC	Imperial Defence College, and
idc	Passed the Imperial Defence Course (later rcds)
JSAWC	Joint Services Amphibious Warfare Centre (or Course)
JSSC	Joint Services Staff College, and
jssc	Passed the Joint Services Staff Course
KBE	Knight Commander of the Order of the British Empire
KCB	Knight Commander of the Order of the Bath
KCMG	Knight Commander of the Order of St Michael and St George
KCVO	Knight Commander of the Royal Victorian Order
KE VII	HMS *King Edward VII*
KG V	HMS *King George V*
(L)	Electrical
LCA	Landing Craft (Assault)
LCS	Light Cruiser Squadron
LST	Landing Ship Tank
MCM	Mine Countermeasures
1MCM	1st Mine Countermeasures Squadron
MDG	Medical Director General
ML	My Lords (of the Admiralty)/My Lords
MMS	Motor Minesweeper
MSS	Minesweeper Squadron
MoD	Ministry of Defence (refers to the whole organization or to the

	central staff)
MoD(N)	Ministry of Defence (Navy), since 1964 a part of the whole MoD
(N)	Navigating specialist
NAD	Naval Air Division (of the Naval Staff, in the Admiralty)
NA&WI	North America & West Indies
nadc	Completed course at NATO Defence College (Rome)
ndc	Completed course at National Defence College (formerly jssc)
NAS	Naval Air Squadron
ND	Navigation and Direction (combined (sub-) specialization)
NL	*Navy List*
NLO	Naval Liaison Officer
NOIC	Naval Officer in Charge
OiC	Order in Council
OOQ	Officer of Quarters (in charge of a battery of guns, or a turret (usually of Lieutenant's rank))
PC	Privy Councillor
pce	Passed all the elements of ship command examinations
PoW	Prisoner of War
PoW	HMS *Prince of Wales*
P&RT	Physical and Recreational Training
psc (or, after 1965, psc(n))	Passed the (Naval) Staff Course
psm	Passed the Army Staff Course
PWO	Principal Warfare Officer
PWO(A)/(C)/(N)/(U)	A PWO who has sub-specialized in Above Water Warfare, or Communications (including Electronic Warfare), or Navigation, or Underwater Warfare, or a PWO (basic) who is in charge of that Section of a warship's weapons systems
QE	HMS *Queen Elizabeth*
R-A(D)	Rear-Admiral (Destroyers)
RCDS	Royal College of Defence Studies, and
rcds	Passed the Royal College of Defence Studies (previously idc)
RHA	Royal Horse Artillery
RIM	The Royal Indian Marine – a successor to the old navies of the East India Company, and a forerunner of the –
RIN	Royal Indian Navy
RMFVR	Royal Marine Forces Volunteer Reserve
RNAS	Royal Naval Air Station
RNC	Royal Naval College (Greenwich, Dartmouth (1905–1954) or Osborne (1903–1920)
RNEC	Royal Naval Engineering College (Keyham to 1946, Manadon, 1946–1995)
RNH	Royal Naval Hospital
RNlN	Royal Netherlands Navy
RNLO	Resident Naval Liaison Officer
RNO	Resident Naval Officer
RUSI	Royal United Service Institute (an old-established 'think-tank')

S	Supply and Secretariat Branch/Specialization
(S)	Signals specialist (later Communications)
SAC	Supreme Allied Commander
SACLANT	(NATO) Supreme Allied Commander, Atlantic (always a USN Admiral; his deputy is always an RN Admiral)
(SD)	Special Duties – an officer on the Special Duties List, who had been promoted from the Lower Deck
SEAC	South East Asia Command (WWII, 1942–45)
SM	Qualified Submariner
SMAC	Short Miscellaneous Air Course
SNO	Senior Naval Officer
SOO (or SO(O))	Staff Officer Operations
SSN	Nuclear-propelled attack submarine
STANAVFORLANT	Standing Naval Force, Atlantic, a NATO squadron at immediate readiness
(T)	Torpedo specialist
(TAS)	Torpedo Anti-Submarine specialist
TB	Torpedo Boat (the forerunner of TBD)
TBD	Torpedo Boat Destroyer
TL	Their Lordships or Their Lordships' (the Board of Admiralty)
TNA	The National Archives (Kew)
tp	Graduate of the Empire Test Pilot's Course
TSR	Torpedo Spotter Reconnaissance
UKHO	United Kingdom Hydrographic Office (successor to the Hydrographer of the Navy)
V&A	HM Yacht *Victoria and Albert*
VCDS	Vice-Chief of the Defence Staff
VCNS	Vice-Chief of the Naval Staff
VE Day	Victory in Europe Day (8 May 1945)
V/S	Visual Signalling (flags and signal lanterns)
WESTLANT	(NATO) the Western Atlantic Area
W/T	Wireless Telegraphy
X	A member of the Seaman Specialization (formerly Executive Branch – also known, ironically or bitterly, as 'the master race'!)

Directions on the use of the CD can be found on page vi.